Door to Door Sales

The ULTIMATE guide to making up to £1,000 per week as a Self Employed Canvasser

Andrew Wild

Copyright © 2016 Andrew Wild

All rights reserved

No part of this publication may be reproduced or distributed in any form or by any means, or stored in any database without the prior permission of the publisher

TABLE OF CONTENTS

INTRODUCTION vii

CHAPTER 1 TOOLS OF THE TRADE 1

Fear of Loss 1

Sheep Factor 4

Indifference 4

Imprinting 5

Stroking Ego 6

Third Party Story 6

Building Credibility 7

Visual Aids 8

Body Language/Tone of Voice 9

Self - Image 10

CHAPTER 2 TYPES OF PROSPECTS 13

The Uninterested Prospect 15

The Interested Prospect 16

The Happy/No Need Prospect 16

The Fearful Prospect 17

The Sceptical Prospect 17

The DIY Prospect 18

The Know – It -All Prospect 18

The Awkward/Stubborn Prospect 19

The Negative Prospect 20

The Rude Prospect 20

The Domineering Prospect 22

CHAPTER 3 WORKING THE TERRITORY 23

Types of Territory 25

No Soliciting Signs 28

Working Hours 28

Law of Averages 29

CHAPTER 4 TRAITS OF A GOOD CANVASSER 33

Attitude 33

Self-Motivation 37

Knowledgeable 40

Organised 40

Genuine/Trustworthy 41

Likeable 42

Empathetic 44

Enthusiastic 44

Believe in Your Product 45

In Control 45

Not Be Afraid to Ask for The Sale 46

Not Full of Excuses 46

A Saver – Not Just a Spender 47

CHAPTER 5 WHY PEOPLE BUY/DON'T BUY 49

CHAPTER 6 THE SALES PITCH 59

CHAPTER 7 OVERCOMING BLOCKS/OBJECTIONS 79

I Am Not Interested! 81

I Am Busy! 85

Are You Selling Something? 85

Is This About Switching? 86

I'm Happy as I am! 87

I Need to Speak to My Partner or Son/Daughter 88

I Need to Think About It. 89

Can You Leave Me A Leaflet/Business Card? 92

I Can't Afford It. 93

I Do Not Buy at The Door! 93

CHAPTER 8 TEN DEADLY SINS **95**

CHAPTER 9 A DAY IN THE LIFE OF A CANVASSER **101**

CHAPTER 10 STORIES FROM THE FIELD **111**

The Nutter Across the Road 111

The Bully Policeman 112

The Loser with The Pretend Bad Leg 112

The Angry Boyfriend 113

The Hyper Kids 113

The Idiot with A Camera 114

Foot Through the Ceiling 114

The Prospect Who Thought Free Panels Were a Rip Off 115

The Moody Man in The Street 116

Prospect Who Just Couldn't Believe It Was Free 117

Prospect Who Thought That He Could Get Solar Panels Cheaper Than Free 118

Prospect Who Said, "No" To Saving Over £700 A Year On His Telephone Bill 118

CONCLUSION **121**

INTRODUCTION

At a time of increased competition for jobs and high unemployment, working as a self – employed canvasser can offer an excellent way to make a living as well as giving you total flexibility over your income and your working hours. Perhaps you are only looking at doing canvassing on a short-term basis, or perhaps you have given up on ever getting a "proper" job or simply don't want one. Either way, you can earn thousands as a canvasser – far more than the majority of people who you will speak to will ever earn. And unlike other self - employed opportunities that are out there, there is absolutely no financial outlay on your part, making canvassing that bit more attractive. You are a professional doing an important job. You are where it all begins. Without you going out there and facing the rejection and hardship that goes with any sales job, nothing else happens. All other jobs within your company are reliant on sales. Without sales no company can survive! This includes many of your prospects' places of work. Yet very few people are prepared to attempt going door to door. Many people think that it is an incredibly hard way to earn a living, and many could not face the rejection that you will inevitably incur, but if you follow the rules that this book teaches you, then working as a canvasser can be a very lucrative way to make a living.

Unfortunately, there is still a stigma attached to those that canvass. There are a lot of people who like to feel vastly superior and view canvassers, and in fact any sales person, as the enemy who is going to use high pressure to get them to buy something they neither need nor want. This can be with good reason, but can be frustrating for the genuine canvasser who is just trying to make an honest living. It is like calling all builders, "cowboys" and all policeman, "bent coppers." Obviously, this is not the case, and likewise, it is not the case about the canvasser either! But unfortunately no matter how honest you are, some people will just not change their perception about canvassers, which makes canvassing that bit more challenging.

Canvassing is also good from the customer's point of view - although admittedly not everyone sees it that way! In a world of mass media, many advertisements get drowned out by the sheer volume. As a result, many people are totally unaware of how your product/service could benefit them. Your role as a Self Employed Canvasser is therefore very informative, and it is a very effective and personal way to communicate what's on offer.

Finally, canvassers are excellent from the company's point of view. It enables companies to get their message across to target customers in an incredibly efficient way. The traditional canvasser would go around peddling books or other household items door to door, but now if you look on the internet, there are many canvassing jobs from all sorts of different companies, from delivering food boxes door to door to home improvements. By sending canvassers door to door, it not only enables companies to target specific areas and qualified prospects, but they only need to pay for results, making it a highly cost-effective way for them to gain new customers.

This book has been divided into ten chapters, which I suggest you read in chapter order.

In Chapter 1, you will learn the tools of the trade and how they can be used to help you get the sale.

In Chapter 2, you will learn about the different types of prospects that you will encounter and how to effectively deal with them.

In Chapter 3, you will learn about the different kinds of territory and how to work them in the most efficient manner.

In Chapter 4, you will learn about the traits of a good canvasser and how to develop some of those traits.

In Chapter 5, you will learn about why people buy and the different motives behind a buying decision.

In Chapter 6, you will learn about the structure of the sales pitch.

In Chapter 7, you will learn how to deal effectively with any blocks or objections that you are likely to encounter.

In Chapter 8, you will learn what I think are the ten deadliest of sins when canvassing.

In Chapter 9, I give you an example of a day in the life of a canvasser pitching free solar.

And finally, in Chapter 10, I share with you some of my most memorable experiences from the field.

But before I begin, let me share with you how I first got into canvassing and give you a brief background on the different products I have canvassed over the years.

I first got into canvassing at the age of 28. I had left University 2 years earlier with a 2:1 Honours degree in Business, but I soon realised the degree was not worth the paper it was written on. I never even got a face to face interview – let alone a job! I was therefore forced to go back to what I was doing before going to University, and that was taking various factory jobs – sometimes as a welder and sometimes as a machine operator. I would work all week long as a robot on a production line and end up with a pittance of a wage. I would constantly be looking at the clock wishing time away until it was break time. I would even look forward to going to the toilet just to escape the sheer monotony of being on a machine. I would be ordered to sweep the floor when the machine I was working on broke down – even when the floor was spotlessly clean. As far as the management were concerned, I was getting paid to work and not to sit around! And there would always be some member of the management who liked to exercise their authority on the rest of us.

Then one day in September 2006, I landed my first face to face interview. It was a Sales and Marketing job based in Birmingham. I attended the interview, which was fairly informal. I was just one of about half a dozen others who were interviewed on that day and who were invited to attend an observation day the next day. I was not too sure what the job entailed. All I knew was that I was to be representing a phone and broadband company.

The next day, when I attended the observation day, I had a brief introduction about the company that I was to be representing before being partnered up with a team leader who worked at the office. We then both got into someone else's car and drove off. I assumed at the time that we were to be visiting different companies in the area, but I didn't want to ask just in case I was supposed to know. We drove for about 45 minutes before being dropped off by the side of the road. "Ok, what is it we are doing then?" I thought to myself. We then walked onto the street and started knocking doors! "What! This is a door to door sales job?" I thought. No wonder the interviewer was so vague at the interview! And what's more, it was a commission only job! Not really knowing where I was and having no means to get back home, I was forced to stay. However, as the day went on, the person who I was teamed up with seemed very enthusiastic and ended up making three sales for the day – despite the fact it had been raining. So with nothing to lose and everything to gain, I decided to give the job a go. After all, it had to be better than working in a factory!

It was not long before I learnt how to sell for myself, and since that day in September, I have gone on to sell a variety of different products all across the UK.

After selling the phone and broadband, which I did for about 18 months, I moved on to selling subscription television. Here I was required to switch people from other providers, or I would be selling to people who had never had subscription television before and were therefore not used to paying extra money for additional channels. I would sign people up to a 12-month service contract and would also sell them a digital box, which would be debited from their card when I booked the sale in over the phone.

After about 18 months selling subscription television, I went on to sell loft & cavity wall insulation under a Government-backed scheme called the "CERT Fund." Here I was able to offer free insulation to the over 70's and those claiming certain benefits. For those that didn't meet that criterion, they could still get their house insulated at a significantly reduced cost.

Once the "CERT Fund" came to an end, I went on to the "free solar" industry. Here I was required to book people in for a free, no obligation survey to see if their house qualified for completely free solar panels. The way that worked was that people would sign a 25-year lease to have solar panels installed on their roof at absolutely no cost to them in return for free electricity during daylight hours. The company who installed the panels would benefit from a Government-backed scheme called the "Feed in Tariff." The Feed in Tariff would pay the company for every unit of electricity generated from the panels as well as for excess electricity exported back to the National Grid. Now to the ill-informed this would sound like a piece of cake. After all, why wouldn't everyone want the panels if they were free and were going to save them money on their electricity? However, many canvassers would fall flat on their face after mistakenly thinking that they could do it "standing on their head." Unfortunately, there has been a lot of myths surrounding the free solar industry, which some people took as concrete facts. Also, it's funny, but quite often it is easier actually to sell someone something rather than give it to them for free! I have lost count of how many times the word "free" has either not registered or people simply don't believe it!

Once the free solar came to an end due to cuts in the Feed-in Tariff, I briefly went on to do charities, where I would ask people to join a weekly lottery for either £1:00 or £2:00 a week to support the charity. I found this completely different to anything else I had done beforehand. First of all, it was rare that someone would be rude to me, but at the same time, it made me realise how bad some people's attitudes are when it comes to helping others. Some people who I spoke to would be very charitable, and would support all kinds of different charities, whereas others only appeared to care about themselves and their immediate family. It really made me see people in a different light and as a result has made me more charitable!

And finally, I moved on to selling gas and electric for those on prepay meters. Here I was required to switch people from other providers, which would end up saving them anything from £50 to £400 a year. Now logically you would think everyone would change if it were going to save them money! Right? Well, wrong! When dealing with people nothing is as straight forward as that!

All in all, I have knocked thousands upon thousands of doors and have gone through several pairs of shoe leather in the process. I have worked all across England and Wales and have spoken to a variety of people from all different backgrounds. At times, it has felt like an emotional rollercoaster, where I have experienced many highs and many lows. However, I have learnt a lot about selling and dealing with people in general, which is why I have decided to write this book, so that you too, after a little practice, can earn a great living from the profession to which I have now perfected.

CHAPTER 1
TOOLS OF THE TRADE

Just like every other profession, there are tools of the trade that will make your life easier. You would not expect a mechanic to work without his tools nor a builder without his. Similarly, a lawyer would not be able to perform without an in-depth knowledge of the law and the ability to use legal jargon and cross-examining techniques. Therefore, as a canvasser, you will also be armed with an arsenal of tools, which you can use at your disposal. Not all the tools will work on all of the people all of the time. You just need to select the appropriate tool for the type of person who you are speaking to.

Fear of Loss

We have all regretted not making a decision about something sooner rather than later, and as a result have missed out on whatever was on offer. We also tend to want what we think we can't have, and the more we feel others want something, the more we tend to want it. It is for this reason why it is important to have some form of fear of loss in your pitch. With this in mind, there are three kinds of fear of loss that you can use. The first, is you want people to feel that they have already missed out on something good, so you could say something like, "I apologise, but my colleague was in the area last week talking to a lot of your neighbours, but it appears he missed you out." By saying this, it will create a certain amount of interest, and will stir up a certain amount of emotional feeling as very few people would like to feel that they have missed out on something when perhaps all of their neighbours have been seen and took advantage of whatever it is you have on offer. Sure, you'll always get some smart - ass who will say, "good" when you say he was missed out, but for the majority of people it will create a certain amount of interest.

Fear of loss can also be used to create a sense of urgency. Without urgency, many people will tend to procrastinate. On the one side, you will have the prospect wanting your product, so there will be a desire for gain, but on the other side, you will have a fear of failure because they will be afraid of making a mistake - especially if they have had a bad experience in the past. Therefore, to win the sale, their desire for gain needs to outweigh their fear of failure, and a good way to do this is to introduce fear of loss into the equation! So once you have made the prospect want your product, you need to have a timeline on your product so that it creates the emotion of losing out. You can either say there is only a limited number on offer, or you can tell them you only come around every 18 months or whenever, and this may be the last time that someone from your company will be around, which is why you want to see as many people as possible. The point is, is the prospect must not be allowed to think that he or she can have your product anytime they feel like having it. If they do, then there is no need for them to make an immediate decision; as a result, their fear of failure could very well outweigh their desire for gain, meaning they will reject your offer.

Finally, you can use fear of loss by telling people that they need to qualify to have your product. If something comes too easy, then people tend not to value it the same. So rather than try and persuade people to have your product, you instead turn the tables around and assume everyone would have your product if they could, but it is up to **you** to decide if they can have it. In other words, it's not available to anyone that says, "yes."

When I was booking people in to have a free survey to see if they qualified for free solar panels, I would tell them that we only come around every 18 months and that I am filling in the surveyor's diary for surveys we are doing in the area over the next ten days. I would then go on and explain how my colleague had missed them out last week, but that we still had a handful of slots left in the surveyor's diary. I would even have a list of names and addresses in front of me so that people could visually see that I already had a fair few names and addresses down. I would then explain that the survey is to determine if they qualify, which was true and that we would let them know approximately ten days later as to whether they can have the panels or not.

And when I was selling subscription television, I would be selling the customer a digital box as well as a 12-month service contract. So to fear of loss them, I would tell them that we were offering the boxes at half price. Therefore, if they wanted to take advantage of the offer, they would need to agree then and there. Sure, they could have got involved at a later date, but they would have to pay full price for the box.

It is important that you create the fear of loss before an objection arises. If you were to go through your whole pitch, then at the end when they said they need to "think about it," it would not sound genuine if you were to tell them that you only have so many left. Also, fear of loss will only work if someone wants what you have to offer. Therefore, unless you have created a certain amount of buying desire, fear of loss will have absolutely no impact on them what so ever. Instead, they will say something like, "fine, well I'll just take my chances."

Sheep Factor

Sheep factor can be one of the most powerful weapons in your arsenal. It can make all the difference as to whether you win the sale or not. Nobody would like to think that they are the only one who has decided to get involved. Whereas if lots of people get involved, then whatever it is that you are doing, it must be good. In other words, people will quite often rely on the decisions of others rather than on their own. After all, everyone in the area cannot possibly be stupid! It is purely safety in numbers. So just like sheep have a herding instinct, as they feel safer in large numbers as opposed to being by themselves, people will also feel far safer if they think a lot of their neighbours are also getting involved. Therefore, you need to say things like: "so what we have been doing for a lot of your neighbours," or "so the reason why a lot of people are getting involved is that of XYZ." For example, when doing the gas/electric for those on pre-pay meters, I would say something like: "So the reason why everyone is getting involved is that it will reduce the cost, meaning more money in people's pocket where it belongs. So all that happens now is we will contact your existing supplier, just like we are doing for everyone else. We will then send you a new key and card, which you will receive in approximately three weeks time, just like everyone else. Once you have your new key and card, you can then top your meter up at the same shops as you do now, just like everyone else will be able to." So as you can see, I have used "sheep factor" several times, which is what you need to do. By doing this, it will imprint it on the prospect's mind that everyone is getting involved, and as a result, you have a far greater chance of winning the sale.

Indifference

Acting indifferent is a great tool to use because it will make you come across as not desperate and not like a typical salesperson.

If you act too desperate or anxious to get the sale, the prospect can become suspicious and may feel that all you care about is your commission. Repeatedly saying things like, "it's up to you" when presenting your product is an excellent way to show indifference. You are only telling them what you have done for many of their neighbours and if they want to benefit too, then great, but if not, then it's no big deal. By doing this, it will make them feel less pressured, and they will feel that they have made the decision for themselves.

Acting indifferent when the prospect first opens their door is also a good idea because it will help to relax them from their initial tense state. You must adopt the attitude that you are doing them a favour and not the other way around. Therefore, act indifferent and not desperate! But remember: acting indifferent is just an act; you should always be eager to get the sale!

Imprinting

Imprinting is designed to influence the subconscious mind of the prospect, which will help people make buying decisions that will benefit them. So as seen above in "sheep factor," you mention how everyone else is getting involved at least 3 – 4 times throughout your pitch.

Another way that you can use imprinting is by saying "today" several times throughout your pitch. So for example, you say, "what we are doing today for everyone," and "so all we are doing today," etc. By doing this, you will imprint it on the prospect's mind that it is happening today - not tomorrow or next week, but today!

You can also use imprinting by saying things like: "when you have your walls insulated, not only will you be saving money on your energy bills, but your home will also be more comfortable too!" Or you can say, "you are just one of many people getting involved." These are simply subtle suggestions where you are using assumptive language and are talking as if they have already made the decision to have your product.

Stroking Ego

A lot of people like to feel that they have some form of worth and that their opinion matters. They like to believe that they are intelligent people and make rational decisions and are respected by others. Therefore, a great technique to win the prospect over is to stroke their ego. You can stroke their ego by admiring a possession they already have, like their car on the drive, or you could show appreciation for their apparent knowledge. So you could say things like: "you sound as if you know what you're talking about." Or, "from the sounds of it, you are quite knowledgeable in this area." Or you could say, "well I'm sure you're an intelligent person." Even if you know that what they are saying is wrong, it is not up to you to just come right out and point that out to them as you don't want to make them feel stupid! You need to be more diplomatic!

Third Party Story

What you are doing here is telling a story of a third party who has had a positive experience buying your product but were apprehensive at first. For example, you could say things like: "I've just been speaking to someone down the road, and he initially had the same fears as yourself. However, he decided to go ahead anyway and over the past 18 months he has saved X amount by switching to us." Or you could say things like: "yes I can understand that you do not watch much television. In fact, I have just been speaking to a gentleman down the road who said the same thing. The reason he said that he doesn't watch much television is because quite often there is nothing much to watch. However, the reason he has decided to get involved today is that not only is he now going to get far better channels to watch, but he is also going to receive a far better signal, meaning a clearer picture." Or when saving people money, you can say things like, "I've just managed to reduce the cost of a gentleman's gas/electric bill by about £200 per year. There was also another lady in the next street who will now be saving approximately £150 per year on her gas/electric." Therefore, by doing this you are making people want a slice of the action, and you are always giving a reason as to why others are getting involved as opposed to saying why they should get involved.

You can also use third party stories to help create dissatisfaction with a prospect's current situation. For example, you could say, "I have just been speaking to a few of your neighbours in the area, and they also have the product you have, but they are finding that their broadband is slow and quite often cuts out." So what you are doing here is highlighting a problem with their existing supplier, which you know to be a common problem, but you are telling it through what other people are saying. Since it is not you that is saying this, they cannot get all defensive with you for criticising the product that they currently have. When I was selling subscription television to those that only had free channels, I would quite often say, "a lot of your neighbours have been complaining that there is nothing much to watch on television and that they get a poor signal through their aerial." Because this was such a common problem, most people would secretly agree with it, meaning I was in a better position to offer a solution to their problem.

Building Credibility

Building credibility with the company you are representing is extremely important because it helps alleviate the fear that the prospect often has when making a buying decision.

You can build credibility in several ways: you can mention any awards that your company may have won, or how many years they have been in business. Or you could mention how many customers your company has. Being honest will also build credibility. Do not just say what you think they want to hear because they will pick up on this and will come to the conclusion that you will say anything to get the sale. If there is a downside to your product, then by all means mention it to the prospect, but make it seem relatively insignificant. By doing this, you will come across as someone who they can trust. As a result, they are more likely to buy from you.

Visual Aids

Having some form of visual aid will prove to be beneficial to you for two main reasons: firstly, some people take things in easier by visually seeing something as opposed to simply hearing you talking about it; and secondly, having a visual aid will take some of the spotlight off yourself. I would always have either a pitch card or a company brochure to hand so that I could show the prospect. If the company that you represent does not provide you with any material, then you can easily make up a pitch card by using photo editing software and taking the finished piece to a library to get laminated in A4 size.

Therefore, rather than just talk, I would show the prospect the brochure or pitch card and read a little what was said. By doing this, it would enable them to take in what I was saying, and it would also make what I was saying sound more believable. For example, when doing the free solar, I would read the first paragraph in the brochure, which explained why the solar panels were free. I would also turn to the section in the brochure where it addressed some of the myths associated with free solar. By doing this, it enabled me to come across as more credible in the eyes of the prospect.

Having a brochure/pitch card to hand is also very effective when dealing with blocks/objections as described in Chapter 7. You use it as a tool to lower the prospect's guard. By physically putting your brochure/pitch card away in your folder, you are signalling that you are no longer attempting to sell the prospect anything, meaning they can lower their guard.

Body Language/Tone of Voice

The use of body language and the tone of your voice is incredibly important and can quite easily play a big part as to whether or not you get the sale. Imagine you have a dog, and you tell the dog to sit in a very monotone voice and without using any body language. It is unlikely that the dog will obey your order. Now imagine you use the same words, but this time, you point to the floor as you tell the dog to sit. You also change the tone of your voice to a stern tone. The dog is now more likely to obey your order - even though you have used exactly the same words. Imagine also if a singer were just to read out the lyrics to a song in a very monotone voice. The song would simply not be brought to life and would fail to stir up any emotional feeling. Therefore, throughout your pitch, you should constantly be varying the tone of your voice. For example, you should sound concerned when you say that it appeared your colleague missed them out last week. And when you are creating dissatisfaction with their current situation, you should lower the tone of your voice. But when you are providing the solution, you can raise the tone of your voice to sound more excited and optimistic.

Using body language on the door with prospects can be useful when referring to their neighbours. You can point down the street at houses to emphasise what you are saying. In fact, when you do this, you will quite often find that the prospect pokes their head out of their door to look down the street!

Body language is also useful when the prospect first opens their door. Instead of standing square on with the prospect, which is confrontational, it is better to stand sideways and approximately a metre away from the door. Not only is this less confrontational, but it shows indifference too! Only after the initial few seconds can you move in closer to perhaps show them your pitch card/brochure.

You can even use your body language to explain how some people you have been talking to in the area have high bills, in which case you would raise your hand up high in the air. Then as you explain that you have reduced people's bills, you will lower your hand, which will help to drive your point home.

Self - Image

It is important that you dress in the right way. The image that you portray to the prospect will have a reflection on the company you are representing. If you look scruffy, or you have a worn out folder, a chewed up pen, etc., then this will portray a negative image in the eyes of the prospect.

As far as dress is concerned, you need to look professional without going over the top. Wearing a suit may come across as too formal, especially when working in lower demographic areas, whereas wearing jeans and trainers will certainly not give a good impression. Personally, I think that it is a good idea to wear dark trousers, a shirt (or jumper in the winter), and a jacket displaying the company logo to which you are representing. If you do not have a jacket with the company logo on, then a plain dark jacket will suffice. You should also make sure that you wear comfortable shoes with relatively soft soles due to the amount of walking you will be doing. By dressing this way, not only will you look relatively smart, but you will not look like a typical salesperson.

CHAPTER 2
TYPES OF PROSPECTS

Understanding the different types of prospects that you are going to encounter is critical to your sales success. It will enable you to determine who to spend your time with in order to maximise your earning potential, and who to spend no time with at all as they will only frustrate you or make you angry with their sheer rudeness and bone-headed ignorant behaviour. In fact, I would say at least 80% of your success in the field will be down to your ability to select suitable prospects and your attitude and energy in the field. The remainder of your success will be down to your pitch and your objection handling techniques.

In the first few seconds of meeting you, the prospect will make some form of judgment about you, but you must also make a judgment about them. You need to determine as to whether or not they are worth spending your time on. Remember, you have many people to see, so you do not need any particular prospect. Therefore, as the prospect first opens their door, you will be observant of their body language and their first spoken words. If they look miserable, ask them how they are before proceeding with your pitch. Sometimes people will not always respond when you ask them how they are, but if they are worth spending any time with, you will see that they will soon relax and become more receptive. You also need to judge how much effort you think the prospect is going to be. Are they worth using your energy on? Or are they just going to be too much effort to deal with?

It is sometimes worth likening prospects to a traffic light system: the greens are happy and positive. They are a pleasure to deal with in that they will not give you any blocks or objections. Most people who adopt the right attitude and who use the right tools, such as sheep factor, etc. would be able to sell to these prospects. The ambers, on the other hand, will give you blocks/objections, which will need turning if you are to secure the sale. These will be the prospects that you will deal with the majority of the time. And finally, there are the reds, which you will be unable to sell to since they are perhaps too rude, too awkward, or too fearful of making a buying decision. They will take too much effort to deal with, and as a result, they will only make you angry or frustrated if you spend too much time with them. What you need to do is determine fairly quickly what state you think the prospect is in. If you do determine that a prospect is firmly in the red state, and is therefore too much effort to deal with, then you must never be afraid to walk away. The problem when working on commission only, however, is that you can sometimes be worried that you will not find any customers and will make no money. As a result, you become desperate and begin to pitch everyone - especially if you have been out knocking doors for 2 - 3 hours in vain.

And finally, you must remember that people are very complicated and can sometimes behave in the most unusual of ways. What may make absolutely no sense to you can make perfect sense to them! Take my father for instance. Since I have known him, he has always been a compulsive hoarder. He will never throw a newspaper away, and as a result, he has collected tonnes of old newspapers over the years. He has also spent thousands of pounds renting a storage unit that he has filled with worthless items. Now logically, his actions make absolutely no sense. Why collect newspaper after newspaper? Why not just read the paper and then cut out any articles of interest? And why keep paying rent on a storage unit only to have it filled with worthless items? It makes no sense! Only a trained psychiatrist would be able to have an understanding of this most unusual of behaviour. But you are not a psychiatrist - you are a canvasser, so do not over analyse why people behave the way that they do. If you do, it will only drive you crazy! Trust me: I have been down that road many a time!

Below is a list of the main types of prospects that you will encounter when going door to door. Some prospects will fit directly into a particular category whereas others may be a mixture of two or more categories, but there will usually be a dominant characteristic that you should be able to notice fairly quickly.

The Uninterested Prospect

These prospects may politely listen to you, but they are not digesting what you are saying since they are not really interested. You can recognise them from their body language, and sometimes you can sense that they are trying to interrupt you, but they are too polite to do so. They do not look interested and sometimes they are not even looking at what you have to show them. Unfortunately, they have made their mind up from the start that they either do not want what it is you have, or they are not going to sign anything then and there. If you have made an effort to create interest, and they are still showing no signs of interest, then it's best just to close them early to avoid wasting time.

These prospects may also tell you that they will "think about it" before you have had a chance to finish your pitch. What they are really saying is: "I am not interested, so please go away!"

The Interested Prospect

These prospects are a pleasure to deal with. They listen to you, they do not interrupt you, they do not give you any blocks, and they seem interested in what you are doing. Sometimes they will have already established the need for themselves and may have even thought about getting your product. When a prospect is interested, they will sometimes lean on their door frame as you are talking to them since they are in no rush to go back inside. They will also quite often ask you questions as they are interested in your offer but just need more information before committing. As long as you answer their concerns, then they should be happy to go ahead. With these prospects, it is always a good idea to compliment them when they ask you a question by saying, "that's a good question. I'm glad you asked." By complimenting them, you will encourage them to ask more questions so that you can flush out any concerns they may have. All in all, they are a pleasure to deal with and will most likely be a customer.

The Happy/No Need Prospect

These prospects will listen to what you have to say since they are not rude, but they are happy with their current provider and see no need to change - even though they may be paying slightly more. Perhaps they have a sense of loyalty because they have been with their current provider for many years. In any case, they do not feel any dissatisfaction with their current situation and therefore feel no need to change. If you have made an effort to create dissatisfaction through your pitch, as described in Chapter 6, and you have tried to turn the objection twice, and they still say they are happy, then forget them as they are clearly a "red prospect" and are therefore not worth your time and effort.

The Fearful Prospect

These prospects are either fearful of making any decision - no matter how small that decision may be, or they are just afraid of change. These are the prospects who will ask you for a leaflet, will say they need to "think about it," or they will tell you they need to speak to someone else before making a decision. If you have presented everything correctly to the prospect, and have turned the objection twice, as described in Chapter 7, and they still give you the same objection, then you should forget them. Unfortunately, they are crippled by fear and are therefore a "red prospect." You must remember that anything you canvass door to door will be something people should be able to make a decision about relatively quickly since it's saving them money, or it's a minor investment on their part. But I am afraid that some people are so fearful of making even the most minor decisions, like saving money on their utilities! You could save someone £300 on their electric bill, and they will tell you they want to "think about it," or will say "I need to ask my partner." Sure, you'll be thinking to yourself that this person is crazy, or perhaps they have misunderstood you, but if they are fearful of changing or don't trust you, then they simply won't do it - no matter how much you say they will benefit. Whereas you could speak to someone else who will only save say, £50 and they will go ahead. There isn't any logic involved! It's just the way it is, I'm afraid. What's important is that you recognise it, accept it, and move on!

The Sceptical Prospect

These prospects are just so suspicious about everything. If your product is free, like it was when I was doing the free solar, they will just not believe you. And no matter what you do, including writing everything down in black and white, they will still think that there must be a "catch." I am afraid these prospects are a waste of time, because even if they do go ahead, there will be a good chance they will cancel on you. Yes, you can perhaps "fear of loss" them by telling them they need to qualify for your product rather than just say, "it's free," but I wouldn't spend too much time with them. Again, you will have different levels of scepticism. The super sceptics are the reds, which you have no hope selling to, but the ambers are only slightly sceptical, meaning you can win them over if you can gain their trust.

The DIY Prospect

These prospects will tell you that if they wanted it, then they would have already got it themselves, or will tell you that they will look into it themselves in their own time. In reality, there are three reasons as to why they have not already got the product for themselves and will be unlikely ever to do so. Firstly, they are not aware they have a need; secondly, they are unaware of the options available to them to satisfy their need; and finally, even if people have identified a need for themselves, many people never get around to doing anything about it. Therefore, by knocking their door you are not only identifying a need, but you are also providing a solution and are helping them to do something about it. It is probably unlikely you will get this prospect to go ahead, so don't spend much time with them. You can try and "fear of loss" them, but some just want to do it in their own time – no matter. Perhaps they are fearful of making a mistake, perhaps they don't trust you, or perhaps they don't make rash decisions. Either way, forget them and move on!

The Know – It -All Prospect

These prospects like to try and impress either you or their family/friends that they are an expert in whatever it is you are doing - even though in most cases they haven't a clue. With these types of prospects, you cannot just come right out and say they are wrong, even though they are because it will dent their ego. The best way you can deal with these prospects is to agree with them and stroke their ego as described in Chapter 1 while at the same time gently correcting them.

The Awkward/Stubborn Prospect

It can be very frustrating dealing with these prospects because they will not listen to you, but will instead just keep saying they are "happy as I am," or they will immediately shut themselves off as soon as they learn what it is you are selling. When you do come across this type of prospect, you need to try and neutralise them and bring them into a more "amber state" because there is no way that they will listen to you in their present state since they are in defence mode. Therefore, you need to be agreeable, as described in Chapter 7. However, if they still continue to be awkward, then it is best just to close them to save wasting your time. So for example, with the gas/electric, you could ask, "would you like to reduce your gas and electric bill like the rest of your neighbours?" They will then respond by saying, "no," just to be awkward, in which case you should just tell them that you'll leave them to it and then walk off. If they continue talking, don't even allow them to finish their sentence as they will only be spouting a load of negativity. Sure, it can be incredibly frustrating because you know full well that if people would just take the time to listen to you and understand what it is you are doing rather than jump to conclusions, then they would benefit enormously from what you are doing. But what can you do? You really feel like grabbing hold of them and shaking them, but unfortunately, you can't. Instead, you just need to walk away and accept the fact that people will quite often reject your offer without knowing anything about it. If only these people really knew what bad decisions they make!

The Negative Prospect

These prospects just think negative about everything. You will hear nothing but negativity coming from them. They will criticise your company or the product you are selling, and they will give you all sorts of negative reasons as to why they can't get involved. They will say things like: "you can't sell your house with free solar panels on the roof," or "yeah the price will go up in a few months." These prospects are a waste of time as they clearly focus on just negative things and can't see the positives in anything. If a company has had thousands of happy customers but only a handful of unhappy ones, guess who these prospects focus their attention on? In other words, they see the glass as half empty as opposed to half full. However, for someone to buy something they need a sense of optimism: they need to feel they will be better off with your product than without it. Sure, you can try and turn some around and make them see the positives in your product. However, many will be too far gone and will be a "red prospect", so don't spend too much time with them.

The Rude Prospect

It is quite unbelievable how some people behave and what they think is acceptable behaviour - not just when dealing with you on the door, but in life in general. For example, some people can be rude to air hostesses and can even give nurses a load of abuse. It is quite amazing. However, these prospects are in a tiny minority. You will find that most people are decent individuals who are not rude to you and would not even dream of slamming a door in your face. Perhaps the idiots who do that are under the false impression that everyone behaves that way to people who knock their door and therefore think that it is perfectly acceptable behaviour. However, there is no excuse for people to be rude to you - especially since you are friendly towards them.

Sure, I can understand that some people may get fed up with having their door knocked, but that's not your fault. You have only knocked their door and spoken with them once! Besides, you are doing people a favour. If you can save someone a few hundred pounds on their utilities, or if you sell them a product that is going to be of real value to them, then surely you are doing them a favour by knocking their door? But unfortunately, you will always get some people who will treat you like the enemy - even at times when you are there to save them money, so you must depart immediately and spend no time at all with these prospects. They are "toxic people" who have either fell victim to their negative environment, or they may have a very negative perception about canvassers. Either way, you must not argue with them, do not try and reason with them, and do not get upset by them. So if anybody angrily says, "can't you read the sign? I don't buy at the door!" then bin them. If someone angrily says, "come on hurry up, what is it you want?" then bin them. Or when asking someone who their current provider is and they say, "it's none of your business," then again bin them. Just ask yourself: would you treat someone like they are treating you? If the answer is no, then bin them! If they are exceptionally rude from the outset, then don't even bother telling them where you are from or why you are there. Just say something like, "I can see I've caught you at a bad time; I'll leave you to it" and then just walk off. Believe me: you will gain an enormous amount of satisfaction by walking away from these types of prospects and staying in control rather than the prospect being in control and shutting the door on you. Besides, do you actually want them benefiting from your product?

There may be times, however, where some prospects may initially appear to be a "red prospect" as your presence on their doorstep has triggered an emotional reaction, meaning they may give you a block or be unwelcoming. However, they may soon calm down once you have gone past your initial introduction. Therefore, by all means, turn the block, but if they are still rude and unwelcoming, then depart immediately.

The Domineering Prospect

These prospects like to take control. They will interrupt you and tell you (not ask you) to leave them a leaflet, and if they are interested, they will contact you. Or they will try and take control of the conversation by interrupting you and asking you questions like, "is this about switching?" Or "are you selling something?" If you answer those questions, then you will allow them to take control of the conversation, and as a result, you will lose any hope of getting a sale. Chapter 7 deals with how to keep control of the conversation when dealing with these types of prospects.

CHAPTER 3
WORKING THE TERRITORY

If you have never knocked a door in your life, then the idea of going up to a complete stranger's door and attempting to sell them something can be rather daunting. But what you will find, is that once you have knocked your first door, then subsequent doors will become easier and easier. You just need to get yourself out of your comfort zone. Don't worry if you mess up as you probably won't see the prospect again anyway. You can even tell people that it's your first day because some people may go a little easier on you as a result. Then, after a while, you will find that knocking doors becomes second nature.

You must always make sure that you knock the door (or letter-box) as well as ring the doorbell because quite often the doorbell will not work. However, this could potentially be a sale. Also, once you have knocked the door, make sure you look towards the window because sometimes prospects will look out of their window to see who it is and will then pretend they are not in if they think you are a salesperson. But if you look towards the window, you can quickly wave to them and then immediately turn away or else they may tell you to go away or may ask you through the window what you want, which is not ideal.

There will be territories that have been knocked harder than others, particularly on large housing estates. In these areas, you may encounter a lot of resistance, so you need to make the extra effort so that you do not come across like all the other canvassers that have been around.

Quite often when I was doing the free solar, and especially when doing the gas/electric, I would come across a territory where someone from the same company, or a different company, had been around the week before. Now the natural thing for me to have done would be to either move to another area or to lose my attitude. However, rather than move to a new area, which was not always convenient, I would just continue to knock the doors. Quite often I would find that perhaps the previous canvasser did not speak to everyone in the territory due to not working evening hours like I would work. Or perhaps some people were busy when the previous canvasser went around but were not busy when I went around. Either way, I would ALWAYS find sales.

There will also be times when you arrive on territory, and you notice other canvassers from other companies knocking your doors. Sure, this may not be ideal since people living in the area may get fed up having their door knocked twice in a day, but it should still not prevent you from making sales. However, if possible, it would be a good idea if you move to another street nearby and come back another day.

Finally, when you come across apartment blocks, where you have to speak through an intercom, you must never attempt to pitch the prospect through the intercom. If you do, the prospect will more than likely tell you that they are not interested. Instead, you should be as brief as possible so that they let you inside the apartment block. So for example, if you are selling gas/electric, you could say, "It's just about your meter." In a lot of cases, the prospect will just buzz you in, and you can then pitch them properly along with everyone else inside the block.

Types of Territory

You will find that every territory that you work in will have sales in it. It is important you do not pre-judge a territory because this will affect your attitude and in turn, will have a detrimental effect on the sales you do for the day. It is all too easy to go into an affluent area with the attitude that everyone is going to be stuck up; or go into a run-down area and think everyone will have no money, or no bank account for direct debits, etc. Sure, you may come across quite a few but not everyone.

I have worked and sold in all different types of territory, from council areas where there have been a lot of houses boarded up, to very wealthy areas with big driveways and swimming pools. Sure, you have to work these different areas in a different way, but if you adopt the right attitude and work ethic, then you will find sales in all types of territory. You may find that you prefer working some areas to others, which is fine, so long as you learn how to work all the different territories.

Below are the three different types of territory that you will find yourself working in.

Low Demographic Areas (Low Dem):

Working low demographic areas, or "Low Dem," as commonly referred to, can have both positives as well as negatives depending on what type of product you are selling. These areas will have large numbers of council houses and high unemployment levels amongst the residents, so you can catch people in at any time of the day and are great if your product will save them money. People are also generally more down to earth and are quite friendly.

However, these areas will also present their unique challenges. The people living there will usually be rougher than other areas and may not have sufficient funds, or a bank account to buy your product, so you need to qualify early to avoid wasting time. For example, when I was selling subscription television, I would need to phone up the office while in the customer's house so that they could debit from the customer's card a £30 install fee as well as money for a digital box. However, many people did not have the money in their bank, and some did not even have a bank account.

When selling to only private houses, you need to be able to weed out the council houses to save wasting a lot of your time. When I was selling loft and cavity wall insulation and free solar panels, I was only able to book in private houses. Therefore, to save wasting my time, I would try and find out if the council houses had something distinctive about them. For example, sometimes the front door would be different and would look the same as a lot of other houses, meaning it would most likely be a council house. Sometimes the council houses would have vents on the windows or roof, or they would have an outside light near the front door that was identical to other houses. Either way, I would identify which were the council houses rather than knock every single door. In the event I was not sure, I would start my opening line as, "I am just going around all the private houses in the area" in which case the prospect would tell me they were not private. Again this would save me time rather than go through my whole pitch only to find out that they were in fact council. I would also ask the prospect if they knew which houses on the street were private and which were a council house. Quite often they would tell me, so again it would save me valuable time.

Middle-Class Areas (Mid Dem):

These areas will probably be where you spend most of your time in. Keeping up with their neighbours or "keeping up with the Jones's" is common in these areas, so you need to use a lot of "sheep factor."

What's great about working these areas is that there will be a significant number of houses on an estate that you can knock, and they will most likely have bank accounts for direct debits, etc. You can find people in at any time of the day; however, the evening time will usually be the time you pick up the most sales as quite often the husband and wife are at work in the day - especially in newer housing estates where there are a lot of young couples.

High Demographic Areas (High Dem):

These areas comprise of large detached houses with long driveways, double car garages, swimming pools, etc.

Saving money will not be an absolute priority here, but then again nobody wants to waste money. Value for money and prestige will be by far the most important. The downside of working these territories is that you cannot speak to as many people as you would in other territories due to a greater distance between the houses. However, on the upside, these types of homes will not have had their door knocked as often as the other territories because a lot of canvassers tend to avoid these areas. It is important that you act professional and dress well as these people could themselves be professional, whether it be doctors, lawyers, accountants, etc.

No Soliciting Signs

You will find "No Soliciting" signs on people's doors/windows in all types of territory. Personally, I think you should knock every door in your territory - regardless of whether they have a sign or not. The only doors that I would recommend that you don't bother with is when the "No Soliciting" sign has been hand written. In this instance, you know they mean business! However, before knocking doors with no soliciting signs, you should find out if any laws are prohibiting you from knocking such doors.

I remember when I was selling subscription television, and it was on the day of the FA Cup final. I approached this door where there was a huge colourful sticker right smack bang in the middle of the door, which read something like, "We do not buy nor sell at the door. Please do not knock as we are happy as we are. We do not wish to change our gas/electric supplier, we do not want cavity wall insulation, we do not want double glazing, we do not wish to change our religion." Undeterred, I decided to knock the door anyway. When the prospect answered, he made no reference what so ever to the sign on his door, which you will find is quite often the case. As it turned out, I got inside his house and signed him up for the full package. Whereas other doors may have no sign, but the prospect will be rude to you. Therefore, having a sign on the door is by no means an indication as to whether you will receive a negative reception or not.

Working Hours

To make the best use of your time in the field, I believe you need to work different hours to an average 9:00 till 5:00 job. Sure, many canvassers do work only during regular hours and still do very well. But personally, I think it is best if you go around your territory **three times** and at **different times**. I believe a good time to start is about 2:00 - 2:30 in the afternoon and then finish about 7:00 - 7:30 in the evening. That way you can go around your territory in the afternoon till about 5:00, where you will usually be speaking to retired people, housewives (or househusbands), people working shifts, etc. You can then take a break for about half an hour before starting again at 5:30. On a sheet of paper, you should have all the road names and house numbers written down, and you should also have a record of who you have spoken to, who you have made appointments with, and which houses where there was no answer. You can then go back around your territory talking to people who were not in earlier in the day and to any appointments you may have set up from earlier. You can then work a further four to five hours on a Saturday where you can go over all the doors knocked in the week where there was no answer, or to any appointments you may have made. All in all, you will only work about 4 - 5 hours a day and will have one day off during the week to compensate for working on a Saturday. Therefore, you should only work about 20 - 25 hours per week - far less than a typical full-time job.

By working your territory this way, it will not only enable you to work fewer hours as you are speaking to the maximum amount of people in a given time, but it will also make your territory last longer than if you only go around your territory once in the day.

Law of Averages

Whatever territory you work in, or whatever product you represent, sales is still essentially a numbers game. The majority of people will say, "no," no matter how good your product is and regardless of whether or not it costs the prospect any money. Therefore, do not question your ability when you hear so many "no's." After all, you are only looking for a tiny minority of people to say, "yes." As long as you speak to the right amount of people and adopt the right attitude and techniques, as described in this book, then you are pretty much guaranteed to make sales. Where it all falls apart, is when you waste your time with the wrong prospects who you have little hope of ever signing up. In other words, the "red prospects."

Usually, the more people who you speak to, then the more sales you will do. That is why you need to make sure that you move around your territory fairly quickly as you will need to speak to as many people as possible. However, you must not be stressed and out of breath because that way you will not be coming across in the right way on the doorstep. You need to strike the right balance. Yes, you need to speak to lots of people, but you do need to be relaxed when talking to those people rather than stressed thinking that you need to see X amount of people in a given period. Remember, any door could be a potential sale, so you need to put 100% effort into everyone who you speak to - regardless of how many people you have spoken to or how many negatives you may have taken.

The product that you are representing and your own personal skill level will govern the number of people that you will need to speak to in a day. For example, with the free solar, I would typically need to speak to say 30 - 40 people a day. Out of those people, approximately 80% - 90% of people would say "no" in one way or another. They would either say, "I'm not interested," "I don't like solar panels," "I will look into it myself," "I need to think about it," or they would believe in some myth they may have heard. But so long as 10% - 20% of people went ahead, then I would still make good money for the day.

When I was doing charities, I would need to speak to far more people to make any decent money. I would typically aim to speak to about one hundred people a day. Out of that, approximately twenty-five people would tell me they already donate to my charity, twenty-five people would say they support lots of other charities, ten people would say they can't afford it, thirty people would just say, "no," and about ten would say, "yes." Therefore, 90% of people would say, "no" to me in some way or another. By placing people into those categories, it made the job easier because I knew that people would always say the same things. Therefore, providing I just work the numbers and don't get frustrated, then eventually I would come across someone who would say, "yes," and sometimes I would come across a few, yes's in a row.

There will be times when you could be knocking doors for 2 - 3 hours and may take 40 - 50 no's in a row - or even more before you get a single yes. Or you may get a sale early on, and then it goes dead for the next 2 - 3 hours as people are either not answering their doors, they don't qualify, or they are not interested. Sure, you can begin to get fed up and may even want to call it a day and go home, or you may think about moving to another territory, but you MUST resist the temptation to do so! You just never know when the yes's will come. You may get three "yes's" in the space of say half an hour, which will totally turn your day around. In fact, there has been many a time when I have had no sales until the end of the evening, and then I get 3 – 4 sales in all at once, but if I had given up, I would never have found my customers and would have instead spent the whole day taking a load of negatives without making any money. Sure, these days are mentally challenging, and you can begin to question your ability when you are taking so much rejection, but that is just the nature of the game, so you must learn to accept it.

Just remember that every territory you go to, there will always be negatives and non-qualifiers, but there will also be a certain amount of potential sales. Say, for example, you were knocking doors, and there were 100 people on the territory, and say after 3 hours you managed to speak to half of those, but they all didn't qualify or were not interested. As a result, you may decide the territory is a waste of time and move elsewhere. However, the other half who you haven't yet managed to speak to could include your sales. So now that you have moved elsewhere, you will have to start all over again weeding out all the negatives and non – qualifiers. That is why even at times where you are not getting sales, it is still an important time as you are weeding out all the non – qualifiers and uninterested prospects and as a result are getting closer to your sales.

There may also be weeks where at the beginning of the week you struggle, yet near the end of the week you get sale after sale and in only two days can triple what you have done for the rest of the week. That is why you should never give up on your week. You really must have the belief that the sales are there. It is like a game of football: you can be two goals down at half time and then go on and win the game. It isn't over until it's over! Just remember, there is money on the street and potentially a lot of it, so go out there and find it!

CHAPTER 4
TRAITS OF A GOOD CANVASSER

There are certain traits that I believe you need in order to become a good canvasser. Some of these traits will come to you naturally while others will need to be worked on with time and persistence. We have all heard the saying that you have to have the "gift of the gab!" And most people think of salespeople as loud, super confident individuals who will be capable of selling "Ice to the Eskimos." However, that could not be further from the truth! You do not want to come across as the stereotypical salesperson as many people do not trust salespeople and perhaps with good reason. You must remember that people like to buy, but they do not like to be sold to - especially by some sharpie who thinks he has the gift of the gab! Below are what I think are the most important traits of a good canvasser.

Attitude

There is a story of two shoe salesman who went to sell shoes in Africa. When the first shoe salesman arrived, to his horror, nobody was wearing any shoes. Feeling deflated, he told his manager that it was a waste of time as nobody was wearing any shoes! However, when the second shoe salesman arrived, he said to himself, "great! I am going to make a killing as nobody has any shoes to wear!"

You see your attitude is your greatest asset. It will determine how you feel about yourself, and in turn, it will determine how many sales you do. Having a positive mental attitude will enable you to keep going when perhaps others have given up. It will allow you to turn objections better, and your whole demeanour will be better as you appear confident and a happy person. You will also be able to make people see your product in a more positive light rather than focus on all the negatives, which a lot of prospects tend to do naturally.

Unfortunately, we live in a world full of negativity. Every time you turn on the news or open a newspaper, it's full of negativity. Then you have bills, health issues, family problems, etc. Even when you are driving, you can face negativity from all the traffic. And on and on it goes! All this is having an adverse effect on your attitude. Imagine having a car that takes dent after dent. After a while, the car is so badly dented it is scrap! Therefore, you need to prevent yourself getting dented in the best way that you can, and if you do get dented, then you need to get repaired before it's too late! The problem is, is that you may not always be consciously aware that your mind is being dented. As a result, you will do nothing about it and will fall victim to your negative environment. You will feel down, depressed and even angry. Therefore, awareness of this issue is so crucial, so that you can do something about it.

There will be many things that will make you feel unhappy and of course some things you will be consciously aware of. Perhaps it is a negative relationship; perhaps it is negative friends, or perhaps it's your environment that you find yourself in. So whatever it is that is hurting you, you just need to recognise it so that you can take actions to combat it.

Having a positive mental attitude is particularly challenging for the canvasser because not only do you have to endure all the negativity from daily life, but you are also faced with continual rejection and negativity from prospects who themselves have fell victim to their negative environment. It does take mental toughness to be a canvasser. You may have had a tough day and then towards the end of the day, you get some prospect who is rude to you and slams the door in your face. But no matter how hard it may be, you must not allow yourself to get emotionally involved because the field will turn you negative if you allow it. It did for me for a while until I learnt to detach myself from the negativity and think much bigger. Working the field is just a means to an end, and it will build you up to be a stronger and better person.

I find a great way to stay positive is by doing plenty of vigorous exercises, like going swimming or jogging, as it will release negative energy.

Listening to music is also a good idea, including listening to music while you are driving, as it will take some of the stress out of driving. Sometimes it can be a good idea to listen to music in your car for about 20 minutes before you start knocking doors as it will put you in a relaxed state – particularly if you are feeling stressed.

It is also imperative that you do not allow negative thoughts to enter your head, and if you do, you need to think immediately of something positive. That includes not dwelling on negative prospects. Therefore, any negative prospects should be quickly wiped from your mind, and you should not walk down the street saying to yourself what an "ass hole" that prospect was. Well, at least not all the time! Instead, you should treat any negative like water off a duck's back. Then, when you get to the next door, you should take a deep breath and refresh your mind so that you can be in top form on every door and give it your 100%, regardless of how many negatives you may have taken.

Sure, thinking positive may be a struggle at first because the mind does have a natural tendency to think negative, but you do need to battle it. If you think negative, you will fill yourself with negative energy, and as a result, you will feel angry, depressed, or stressed. If you feel angry, depressed, or stressed, then you will look either angry, depressed, or stressed, which of course is not the image you should be portraying to your prospects. Sure, you may feel you will get away with thinking negative, but you won't!

Also, if you have self-limiting beliefs such as, "I would never be capable of earning £1,000 in a week," then you never will. Your subconscious mind is like a computer that will do what it is programmed to do. It cannot differentiate between real or imagined. So whatever you do, just make sure that whatever enters your head is positive! This is especially important just before you fall asleep and when you first wake up in the morning as you are drowsier, and therefore your mind is more receptive. Therefore, it is a good idea to make positive affirmations to yourself during this crucial period, and after time your subconscious mind will take whatever you have told it as fact, meaning your whole attitude will change for the better! This could also include eliminating any fears that you may have acquired throughout your life.

And finally, you need to **accept** the field for what it is. You should accept the fact that many, many people do not make intelligent decisions. You must **accept** that there are always going to be awkward people. You must **accept** that you will come across ignorant people. You must **accept** the fact that you will get the odd door slammed in your face, and you must **accept** that people will say they are happy as they are after you have proven you could save them a lot of money on their utilities. Just **accept** the job for what it is. Just like if you are a mechanic you have to accept getting your hands dirty, or if you are a nurse you are going to have to clean up vomit from time to time. What's important is that you accept the job for what it is. If it was that easy and everyone who you spoke to were nice and friendly and listened to what you had to say, then companies would not need to pay the money that they do. Instead, they could just pay the minimum wage as anyone would be capable of doing the job. Therefore, be thankful that there are awkward and rude people because they are indirectly making you a lot of money, but only if you do not allow them to get to you. So the next time some idiot slams their door in your face, or the next time someone says, "I am happy as I am" once you have proven they could save a lot of money on their utilities, just breathe a sigh of relief that those people exist! And remember, no matter what happens in the field, you will always win so long as you remain positive, yet the negative prospect will always lose as they will have missed out on benefiting from your product.

Once you have successfully "un – dented" your mind, you will feel entirely different. All of a sudden everything will seem possible and achievable rather than impossible and unachievable. You will feel empowered and will feel as if you can move mountains. You will be an unstoppable force! The world will be your oyster! Your mind will work wonders for you, and the positive energy to which you radiate will draw people towards you. Until you truly experience this, you will not appreciate what I am saying. Have blind faith in what I am saying, and after time, depending on how badly dented you are, you will see for yourself! It will be like freeing a wild animal from its cage so that it can fulfil its true potential!

Self-Motivation

You may have heard the phrase: self-employment minus self-motivation equals self-destruction. That is so true when working on a self-employed basis. There is no one telling you that you have to go out to work. You can quite easily get up in the morning and decide just to chill out watching television all day or playing computer games. And if you make the mistake and think of all the negatives that you will inevitably encounter, it becomes all too easy just to say, "sod it; I'll work harder tomorrow to compensate." However, once tomorrow comes, you are likely to feel the same.

When doing door to door, you will quite often find that the hardest door is the car door, but once you begin speaking to people and getting sales it becomes easier and easier. Therefore, on days when you perhaps really feel like not getting out of your car, you do need to force yourself. After all, you will feel a lot better if you make a few sales for the day!

To be self-motivated, you need something to aim for. You need direction because without direction it makes what you are doing day in and day out rather cumbersome. Therefore, you need specific goals to keep you motivated. In other words, you need to think a lot bigger than just knocking doors. Perhaps you want to save up for a new car, or maybe you want to save up for a deposit to buy a new house or pay off your mortgage early. Whatever your goals are they need to be **specific and achievable**. You need to break your goals down to make them achievable. If you were to climb Mount Everest, you would not want to be standing at the bottom looking up at the peak. Sure, that may be your longer - term goal, but first set yourself a short - term goal of climbing to the first marker point or wherever. Similarly, if your goal were to buy a car for say, £10,000 in 6 months' time, you would need to break that goal down. You would need to work out how many sales you need to do per week, how many people you will need to speak to in order to achieve those sales, and how many doors you will need to knock in order to speak to those people.

Personally, I think it is a good idea to set yourself short - term goals and then take a week off. So for example, on a piece of paper, you can write down what you want to achieve over a six-week period. So one week you might use to pay all your bills for the month, another week you might aim to save X amount of money, and so on. These shorter - term goals will help to keep you motivated week after week as each week you have a specific goal that you are trying to achieve while also getting closer and closer to your longer - term goal. And by taking a week off it will enable you to push yourself because you know that every six weeks you will get a week off. This I feel is important to keep you firing on all cylinders. Although you may not work an enormous amount of hours in a week, it is still mentally tiring as you have to deal with a lot of negativity, and you constantly have to think how many sales you have done for the week so that you can hit your goals. By taking a week off, or even half a week off, it enables you to refresh your mind and recharge your batteries for the next six weeks until you take your next week off. It is a case of taking one step back but two steps forward.

Finally, you will need to make sure that you stay **focused** and can work under pressure so that you can hit your goals. Sometimes, for example, you may need a certain number of sales to qualify for bonuses that your company has to offer. You may find yourself out on the last day of the week trying to find those extra few sales to hit your goal. Sometimes you may only need to find just one more customer, and that customer may be worth £200 to you because of the extra payments you will receive in bonuses. But you may be faced with obstacles, which will make hitting your goal that bit more challenging. It may start to rain, you may encounter a large number of non – qualifiers, or there may be scores of awkward prospects, and the day could be drawing to a close, yet you need to stay calm and just focus on getting the job done. Do not allow yourself to get beaten! You must be a fighter and not a quitter! But when you finally hit your goal, you will feel great!

You will also need to stay focused on your longer - term goal too. Quite often people will set themselves goals in the time between Xmas and New Year as for most people it's quite often a dead time, so it is therefore an excellent opportunity to reflect and gather your thoughts for the year ahead. Losing weight or joining a gym is quite often a common goal, yet by the end of January, a lot of people lose sight of their goals as soon as they get back on life's train. Therefore, you need to be strong and resist the temptation of giving up on your goals. You need to be constantly reminding yourself of the reason why you set the goal in the first place and the positive outcome that you envisage by achieving your goal.

Knowledgeable

It is important that you know your product inside out as well as that of your closest competitors. For example, with the gas and electric, you should be aware of the tariffs of all the leading providers. You should also know the positives of your product as well as any negatives. Nobody likes to deal with a poorly informed salesperson. If a prospect was to ask you a question and you did not know the answer, then you need to find out the answer. Just say to them, "that's a good question, to be honest, I do not know the answer, but I'll find out for you." That will give you the respect that you deserve as you are answering people's questions in an honest way rather than just "blagging" your way through the sale.

Organised

Being well organised is important. You are your own boss; therefore, it is down to you to be organised in everything you do. For example, I was incredibly organised when I was doing the free solar. I use to keep a record of all the people who I booked in for a survey, so the next time I was to go to my territory, I would know who I had booked in for a survey, who had cancelled, and who had got installed. Armed with this information, I was able to avoid knocking doors of houses that I had already booked in for a survey. I could also try and persuade those who cancelled to reconsider. And finally, I could refer to the installs when I was speaking to other people living in the area, which would help me gain more sales.

I would also print out several street maps of the town of which I was planning on working, and I would then use Google Earth to check out the territory. With the solar panels most houses did not qualify because they were either too small for the number of panels we needed to fit on the roof, they were facing in the wrong direction, or they had shading issues. By identifying this beforehand on the computer, it would save me time and would allow me to use the best of my time in the field.

Genuine/Trustworthy

Unfortunately, salespeople are perceived by many as untrustworthy, meaning you can sometimes have an uphill task to build that all - important trust. If people do not trust you, then they will not take the risk of buying off you. You can explain things to a prospect as clearly as you can, and you may even show them that they could perhaps save £200 on their gas/electric bill, but they will still not go ahead. They will say that they "need to look into it," or "they never sign anything on the door." You will be saying to yourself, "gee this person is crazy! What the hell is wrong with them? Are they thick or what?" However, you need to understand that the prospect is having to put their trust in you. It is you that is saying it will save them money. It is you who is saying they will be better off with your product than without, but it is you that is also the salesperson who in the eyes of the prospect will say anything to get the sale. That is why asking a few questions about themselves or admiring something that you have noticed in their house can make all the difference. It won't work for everyone because some people will not trust you – no matter what! Sure, it can be very frustrating because you know you are honest and that you are not there to con them. But in a lot of cases, there is nothing that you can do except to move on and forget them.

Another way that you can help to build trust is not to appear too desperate and say everything you think they want to hear. Be honest. If your product is not particularly good in one particular area, then do not pretend that it is. By doing this, you will come across as someone they can trust.

Likeable

The ability to build relationships in selling is essential. You will make very few sales if you rely purely on logic. I by very nature are very logical, so for years, I got very frustrated when dealing with people. I did not see the point in wasting time in building relationships. After all, if I could show the prospect that it would benefit them, then why would they not just go ahead? Well, the answer to that is because people are emotional, and their emotions dictate their actions. Would you buy a product off someone you didn't like, even though you really might like the product? Well, you probably wouldn't and nor would they. Building a relationship will also help you build the all-important trust as described above.

The relationship will be formed from the first few seconds with the prospect. From your smile, your eye contact, and by showing an interest in them, it will trigger certain emotions deep inside their subconscious mind, meaning they will begin to warm to you.

The best way to show an interest in someone is by asking questions about themselves. If there are pets or children on the doorstep, you should not ignore them. Quite often children will speak to you, or will have a toy in their hand, or may be dressed in a funny outfit. You must talk to them a little, or at least acknowledge them. Or if there is a dog, you should ask the owner what his name is, etc. By doing this, you are showing that you are a real person and that you are relaxed and not desperate to get the sale. Imagine how you would feel if someone came to your door and just launched into their pitch, ignoring everything else. You would simply not warm to them!

When inside the house there are plenty of things you can talk about, like pictures hanging on the wall, musical instruments, furniture, etc. You must, however, sound genuine. When relating to people, you should not do it purely to get a sale, but you should be genuinely interested in what you are asking. I remember one time when I was selling phone and broadband, and both the husband and wife were hesitant in making a decision and wanted to think it over. So I stopped selling the product, but instead, I started talking about the piano that I had noticed in their living room. I mentioned that my brother played the piano and asked them what grade they were. That took the tension out of making a buying decision, and after only about 5 minutes of talking about the piano, I closed them again, and this time they decided to proceed. However, there are times when you may have had a tough day and just want to get a sale desperately, so you forget about any relationship building and instead just focus on the job in hand, but this will have a reverse effect on what you are trying to achieve. Therefore, you must take a step back and relax.

Finally, a word of warning: if you get too friendly, then it can become difficult to ask for the sale or turn any objections because you do not want to compromise the relationship that you have just built up. Therefore, to save embarrassment, you politely leave, which of course completely defeats your objective!

Empathetic

You need to show empathy towards your prospects. Understand that making a buying decision can be a nerve-wracking experience. People can also get set in their ways - especially the older generation who have perhaps been with their current provider for many years or have paid their bills by cheque as opposed to by direct debit. Therefore, understand why people do the things that they do. It may make no sense to you, but you must show an appreciation of their worries while telling them that others in the area initially felt the same way but decided to go ahead for whatever reason.

Enthusiastic

Although it is not a good idea, in my opinion, to be overly enthusiastic when the prospect first opens their door, since you need to relax them rather than put them on edge, a certain amount of enthusiasm is always essential. If you cannot show any enthusiasm and get excited about your product, then how can you expect your prospect to get excited? By being enthusiastic, your enthusiasm will rub off on the prospect and as a result, it will help to secure the sale. The last thing you want to do is mope around with the weight of the world on your shoulders, showing absolutely no enthusiasm what so ever, just because you have taken a few negatives.

Believe in Your Product

You should never find the need to use some real persuasive techniques just to get a prospect to say, "yes," and you should never take the attitude that if they say, "yes," they are doing you a big favour. Instead, you should take the opposite approach. You must believe in your product and how it will benefit the customer. It is you that is doing the prospect a favour by knocking on their door and offering them your product. If you never made the effort to knock on their door, then they may continue for years paying more for their gas/electric than they need to, or they may continue for years using an inferior product. That is why you should never be shy about knocking on people's doors. In fact, many of my customers would quite often thank me for calling. Remember, you are not there to con them: you are there to help them, and if you feel that they won't benefit from your product, then you shouldn't sign them up, so you have nothing to feel ashamed about. If they want to believe something different, then that's their problem! At the end of the day, you have good intentions, so remember that and be proud of your product.

In Control

As a canvasser, you need to be in control of the situation at ALL times. You must never allow the prospect to take control of the situation. If you do, you will lose the sale. They will tell you to leave them a leaflet, and if they are interested, they will call you. They will sometimes try to hurry you up when you are pitching them, and they will have you go away repeatedly and come back when it suits them. People do not care about how much hassle they put you through – nor anyone else. It is all about them, which is why you need to stay in control.

Asking questions can help you keep control of the conversation as they demand an answer. Asking questions are very useful if people are acting negative, and you can sense you don't have much time. By asking a question, or a series of questions, it focuses their mind away from being negative and on to answering the question.

Not leaving someone a leaflet when they tell you to will help you stay in control, and instead of rushing through your sales presentation just because they have told you to hurry up, you need to excuse yourself and say you will try and catch them another time when they are not so busy. You will not allow the prospects to dictate to you. It is you who calls the shots! It is you who is in control, so remember that!

Not Be Afraid to Ask for The Sale

As I have stated several times throughout this book, making a buying decision can be a nerve-wracking experience. Therefore, the safer option is for prospects not to do anything and simply carry on as they are. To make the sale, you need to ask for it. You cannot expect prospects to close themselves. It does happen on occasions, but for the most part, it is you that needs to do the closing.

Timing is everything when it comes to asking for the sale. Closing too soon will mean the prospect has not yet reached buying temperature, whereas closing too late and they will begin to cool off and as a result will quite often just ask you to leave them with something. With time, you will get a feel of when it is the right time to close. But usually, once the prospect has agreed with you a few times, then it is usually a good time to close.

Not Full of Excuses

Excuses are like ass holes: we all have them, and they all stink!

What good is it if you come back with no sales but full of excuses? You need to learn to find solutions and not excuses! Sure, I used to come up with all sorts of excuses until I realised that they won't get you anywhere. You will hear things like everyone in the territory was too old, or everyone had no money, or my doors had been knocked the week before, or everyone living in that area was grumpy. Whatever excuse you use it's just an excuse! Learn to adapt and adjust your work ethic if needed. Just don't make excuses! Like Mark Twain, the American author once said: "there are a thousand excuses for every failure, but never a good reason."

A Saver – Not Just a Spender

It is important when working on a commission only basis that you save a little rather than live hand to mouth. By having money saved, it not only takes the pressure off you, but it also covers you for the unexpected, such as adverse weather conditions or being sick. You have to bear in mind that you are running your own business and need to plan ahead accordingly. If you have no funds in your bank, then you will find that working on commission only is a hard way to earn a living as you will have no stability. Sure, when first starting out you may have no funds in your bank, which was the case for me. However, you must quickly build up your account so that you have a nice cushion. That way, it will make you more relaxed in the field as you will not be stressing yourself out thinking that you need to get a certain amount of sales in order to pay the bills.

CHAPTER 5
WHY PEOPLE BUY/DON'T BUY

The simple answer as to why people buy is either because they feel a sense of dissatisfaction with their current situation, or they are looking to satisfy a particular desire.

In many cases when people buy something they will have identified the need or desire for themselves, and as a result, they will actively search for a solution to their problem or desire. However, when going door to door, quite often you will need to create that need from scratch because people will not feel they have a need for your product, or they will not know the solution to their need until they have spoken with you. When I was selling loft and cavity wall insulation, I would quite often have available to me a thermal image of the person's house that showed heat escaping through their walls and loft. By showing the prospect this, it would create that need, which did not exist beforehand. I would then provide the solution to that problem, which of course was insulation.

When looking at the reasons as to why people buy, it is important to distinguish between needs and wants. At the most basic level, a need is something that we all need to survive like, food, water, and shelter. However, we may want a detached house with a nice garden for our shelter, or we may want to eat a fillet steak for our food, but we certainly don't need it - we want it! Similarly, a man with a young family may need a people carrier if he is to transport his family around without using public transport, but he may want a sports car. Or in the dating world, a woman may need a "nice guy," but she wants a "bad boy" as it plays on her nurturing instinct. Neither is good for her. The "bad boy" will hurt her whereas the "nice guy" will bore her. What she ideally needs is a happy medium.

Needs by themselves are not exciting. They are mostly logical reasons for having something as they solve either a real or imagined problem, whereas a want is more of an emotional reason for having something and therefore will satisfy an emotional requirement.

There may be several motivational factors involved in the purchase decision. Some will be rational motives, and some will be emotional, but there will usually be a dominant buying motive. What is important, is that you identify what a prospect's true buying motive is so that you can tailor your presentation in order to try and satisfy that motive. Just be aware that a prospect's true buying motive will not always be obvious!

The six main buyer motives are:

The Desire for Financial Gain - This will include saving people money on their household bills, or increasing the value of their house through home improvements.

Fear of Loss - This will motivate people to buy things like insurance, and as I explained earlier, it will motivate people to take action rather than procrastinate out of fear of losing out.

Comfort & Convenience - This will include making people's homes more comfortable through various home improvements, or by making people's lives more convenient in one way or another.

Security & Protection - This will include guarantees, warranties, etc. If you are dealing with someone who is fearful of making a wrong buying decision, then offering a guarantee or warranty could be a huge motivational factor.

Pride & Prestige - This could be associated with the brand name, or by the product itself. For example, Rolex and Rolls Royce have a very high prestige value.

Satisfaction of Emotion - This will include doing things for the benefit of others, like buying a gift for a loved one, or donating to charity.

So in the case of the insulation, people may purchase the insulation for financial gain because not only will it save them money on their heating bills, but it will also add value to their house through a higher energy efficiency rating. Or, they may buy insulation because it will make their home a more comfortable environment.

With solar panels, there may be three primary motives, depending on the type of prospect. Firstly, it could be for financial gain since they will save money on their electric bill. Secondly, it could be for the satisfaction of emotion because it will make them feel good about themselves since they are using renewable energy and are therefore doing their bit for the environment. And thirdly, it could be the feeling of prestige that they have from having solar panels on their roof.

And when saving people money on their gas/electric, the obvious motive is the desire for financial gain. However, if you can offer a price guarantee, then they may be motivated by the security and protection, which that offers since they don't have to worry about the price going up in a few months' time. Or, if you can offer the prospect a wider range of places where they can top up their meter, then they may be motivated by the extra convenience. For example, some shops don't allow people to top up if they are with certain providers. As a result, they may have to travel further afield to top up, which can be very inconvenient. Therefore, if they can top up at their local shop with your provider, then this may be a real motivational factor for them. In fact, if a product is more convenient and gives the prospect far greater security, this will quite often motivate a prospect more than any financial gain. They may even be prepared to pay slightly more as a result. Therefore, if you come across a situation where there is not much difference in the price, you can perhaps tailor your presentation around these other motives in order to win the sale.

As well as understanding what motives people to buy, it is also worth understanding some of the reasons as to why someone who has a need for your product decides not to buy, and what it's like being a customer faced with making a buying decision.

There are four main reasons why a qualified prospect who has taken the time to listen to your presentation and who has a need for your product will reject your offer:

The first is fear. Unfortunately, fear can hold people back in many ways. The fear of failure will hold people back because if they make the wrong buying decision, it could lead to huge financial loss, which in turn could very well result in emotional dissatisfaction, bringing on feelings of anger, hopelessness, insecurity, etc. This will particularly be a problem if they have had a bad experience in the past. The fear of the unknown will also hold people back because people like familiarity since it brings on a sense of security. However, in many cases, there is nothing to fear but fear itself. Fear is merely the acronym to False Evidence Appearing Real. It is just emotional, yet emotions control people's actions, and it will sometimes cripple them when it comes to making a buying decision.

Secondly, if the prospect's current level of dissatisfaction does not outweigh the initial cost, they may reject your offer. It is for this reason why you must focus your attention on building as much value in your product so that price becomes less of an issue.

You must not make the mistake and think that price is the number one issue in the buying decision unless of course the product cannot be differentiated in any other way. If price were the number one issue, then all your prospects would have the cheapest car available sitting in their driveway. People would sooner pay more for a product if they perceive it to be of better value or less of a risk. As can be seen above, there are other motivational factors other than price, so don't get caught up with the price issue.

Thirdly, habit and inertia will cause people to reject your offer. It can be all too easy for them just to carry on as they are, even though their situation may be less than ideal. After all, it can be better the devil you know! Therefore, unless you can create a level of dissatisfaction that will overcome this, the prospect will reject your offer - especially if they think that there is a lot of hassle involved, which is why you must always make sure that you present your product with minimal of hassle.

And finally, mistakes made on the part of you, as the sales rep, will cause people to reject your offer. To illustrate this, I would like to share with you an experience that I recently had when I was looking at buying a Jaguar sports car. This will highlight how a sale can so easily be lost. I visited four dealers in total, and although I liked the first three cars that I went to see, I did not buy them due to some fundamental errors made by the dealers.

The first dealer who I visited made several mistakes. Firstly, he never showed me all the features and benefits of the car. Instead, he just allowed me to look at the car myself and even allowed me to test drive it by myself. After I had come back from the test drive, I wanted to see what had been done to the car, so I asked to look at the paperwork. But instead of going through the paperwork with me, he just handed me a pile of unorganised papers. I asked him how flexible he was on the price since I did notice that the brake discs were worn and would need replacing shortly. However, the dealer was unwilling to make any price concessions, but instead, he just handed me his business card and told me to go away and think about it.

A couple of hours later, the dealer rang me and said that he had just taken another booking to view the car for the Saturday morning, which was just a couple of days away. He told me that he just wanted to make me aware of this as I was a "local lad," as he put it. However, being in sales myself, I suspected that this was just a ploy to "fear of loss" me into making a buying decision. In any case, I decided to ring some garages to get a quote on how much it would cost to put new discs and pads on the car. I got a quote for approximately £500, so the next day I rang the dealer and explained that I had got a quote for £500, yet he was still unwilling to knock any money off the car. Therefore, I decided that I was not going to buy the vehicle. I did not want to spend a lot of money on buying the car and then have to spend further money on doing the discs. If anything it was the principal of the matter.

On the day that the other person was supposedly going to look at the car, the dealer rang me on my mobile and agreed to knock some money off the car, but he would need a deposit immediately to secure the vehicle. By this time, however, I had already accepted that the dealer was unwilling to reduce the price, and I had therefore already decided in my mind that I was not going to buy the car. I also didn't believe him when he said someone else was looking at the car because why would he even bother to ring me? Why not just sell it to that person instead? So I told him that I could not get him the deposit as I was on my way to work. As I later found out, the dealer did not sell the car - nor did he for some time after.

My experience with this dealer highlights how a sale can be easily lost. Firstly, it was a mistake not coming on a test drive with me. He needed to show me the various features and benefits of the car, as being unfamiliar with the car, I did not know how to use various features that the car had. He also made a mistake by not going through the paperwork with me. By simply handing me a pile of unorganised papers, it was hard for me to see what work had been done to the car and when. It would have been far better if all the paperwork had been neatly placed in a folder, and the dealer went through it with me. Finally, not closing me then and there was a huge mistake! Sure, he did not want to put pressure on me, but he could have still closed me without appearing to exert pressure on me. Remember, I am at my hottest now. I have just come back from test driving the car and have therefore built up a certain degree of emotional attachment towards the car. I am sitting in the office looking out of the window at this shiny car sitting there on the forecourt, but I need closing! By letting me leave without buying then and there, it gave me a chance to cool off. It is like taking water off a hot stove. I now go away and begin to think of all the negatives and the reasons why not to buy the car. I also start noticing other cars for sale elsewhere. The initial impulse is starting to wear off. Therefore, by the time the dealer decided to lower the price, I had cooled off sufficiently to reject the car. The offer had come in too late!

The funny thing is, is that I would have probably bought the car if the dealer had initially asked more for the car, but reduced the price to what he had it advertised at because psychologically I would have been happy at having some money knocked off.

The location of the second dealer was much further away than the previous one, so I rang the dealer to see how much he would take for the car. He immediately gave me a reduction over the phone, which was a big mistake. He would have been better off just saying that the price may be flexible, but by giving an actual reduction it lost its effect. When I went to look at the car, I had totally forgotten what the original price of the car was, but instead, I was thinking of the reduced price. In other words, I had by now taken the discount for granted and was thinking of reducing the price still further. When I came back from test driving the car, I went into the office to look through the paperwork. However, I was undecided as to whether to buy the vehicle or not. There were a couple of things that I was not quite sure about, but I could have still so easily gone either way. I was 90% there, but I needed closing. It is much like a runner who needs that last little spurt of energy to get over the finishing line and win the race. However, the dealer was unable to push me over the edge since he had already given the price reduction over the phone. He had also not made it easy for me to buy the car because he did not offer free drive away insurance, which a lot of dealers offer. Therefore, I would need to arrange insurance to drive the car home, yet it was getting late, and I didn't feel like looking for insurance, so I decided not to buy the vehicle.

The third dealer who I went to see lost the sale from the beginning because he made the mistake of prejudging me. When I went to look at the car, I arrived in an old banger, which someone temporarily lent me, as the car that I normally drove - a classic VW Beetle was currently having some work done. When I was talking to one of the sales reps, I happened to turn around quickly and noticed the owner of the garage nodding behind my back as to say, "no" to the sales rep. The only possible reason that I can think for that was that the owner saw me arrive in the old banger and therefore made the assumption that I would not have the money to buy the car and that I was just a dreamer/ time waster. Because of this, the dealer made no effort to sell me the car and did not even offer to take me for a test drive. As a result, I obviously did not buy the car.

A couple of days later, I finally bought my Jaguar sports car and for slightly more money than all the other cars. And why did I buy it? Well, the answer is simple: the dealer made none of the mistakes of the other dealers but instead sold it to me like a professional!

So as you can see from the above examples, there is sometimes a very fine line as to whether someone buys from you or not. It must be noted, however, that price reductions cannot create buying desire. If someone does not want what it is you are selling, then a price reduction will have little effect.

Also, offering a price reduction is by no means the only way that you can push someone over the edge so that they make a buying decision. Another effective way, which the first two dealers failed to do, was to recite all the benefits of the car to make me realise that I am unlikely to find a better car elsewhere. In other words, they would be building value to justify the price and to push me over the edge. Alternatively, if I happened to be with either a friend or family member who encouraged me to buy the car, then this could have made all the difference because opinions of others quite often matter. Finally, creating fear of loss in the correct manner could have pushed me over the edge. But as it was I had to make the decision all by myself without that final push over the edge. As a result, I took the easy and safe option and did nothing.

Although buying a car is a much greater purchase than what you will typically sell door to door, the principles are still the same. You still have to make the effort to show people the features and benefits of your product. You must never prejudge because you never know who your customers might be. You must hold back giving any discounts until right at the end when they need that final push over the line. You must satisfy all of the prospect's concerns. You must make the purchase hassle free. You must recite the benefits of your offer to build the value in your product. You must use "fear of loss"; and finally, you must close at the right time and not allow the prospect to go away and "think about it" as it will be unlikely you will ever hear from them again if you do.

CHAPTER 6
THE SALES PITCH

The first thing you need to understand is that there is no "perfect sales pitch." Some people you simply cannot sell to - no matter what! Even if you were going around giving away a car worth £60,000 for free, you would still have people say, "I'm not interested!" Or, "can you not read the sign? I do not buy or sell at the door!"

Your pitch should not sound like a pre-rehearsed sales pitch because if it does, the prospect will feel as if they are being sold to. It will also make your job incredibly boring if you pitch everyone like you are a robot. Instead, you need to act as naturally as possible and take a more conversational approach while at the same time having that all important structure of your pitch: Introduction, Fact Find, Presentation, Close, and Consolidation. This structure is important as each stage of the pitch will lead you closer and closer to getting the sale. Sure, you may get put off track if the prospect throws an objection or block at you, but what's important is that you deal with any objections/blocks and get back on track as quickly as possible.

One of the mistakes that a lot of canvassers make - including myself when I first started doing door to door was to speak too fast and have no pauses in my pitch. That was due to nerves and a lack of confidence. I would rush through my pitch so that I could get the pitch out as quickly as possible before the prospect had a chance to give me a negative. However, that was a big mistake because people have limited attention spans, meaning they will be unable to absorb what you are saying if you talk too fast. In fact, the other day a girl stopped me on the street trying to get me to sign up to a charity. However, she spoke so fast that I hadn't a clue what the charity was about or how much she wanted from me. Instead, I just switched off, and as a result, I didn't sign up. It is therefore far better that you speak slowly and clearly so that the prospect can understand what it is you are saying because if they don't understand what you are saying, then they will simply reject your offer without bothering to ask you for clarification. You should also pause during your pitch. For example, when you ask the prospect how they are, you should pause and wait for them to reply rather than interrupting them and proceeding with your pitch.

The first part of your pitch is the **Introduction**. Remember, you are there to communicate the features and benefits of your product, but to do that you have to get past first base. If the prospect just shuts the door in your face or shuts themselves off as soon as you have introduced yourself, then you have no hope of making any sales.

It is worth putting yourself in the prospect's shoes. They may have just sat down after a long day's work, or may be preoccupied doing something else when all of a sudden they hear a knock at their door. As they open their door, there in front of them is a complete stranger. It is only natural that they might be slightly on edge when they first open their door. Therefore, the last thing that they need is some eager, overly excited canvasser introducing themselves and launching into their pitch. Think what you would do. It is all too easy just to say you are "not interested" as you are not interested in listening to a load of spiel!

Instead, you should act like "the wolf in sheep's clothing."

Therefore, rather than acting all sales - like and enthusiastic when the prospect first opens their door, you need to act very indifferently. Perhaps you could have your back turned, or perhaps you could be looking down at your paperwork as if you are busily distracted by that. You could then look up and say something like, "sorry I was a million miles away there!" Or simply say, "Hi are you alright?" But not "hi how are you?" as it sounds too scripted. Also, smile as you will come across as friendly, which will help the prospect warm to you. You may even want to use an icebreaker before telling them why you are there. For example, if you smell something cooking you could say, "that smells nice! It looks like I've come at the right time!" Or use a cue from whatever else you may have noticed, like a pet or an outfit that they might be wearing.

By taking this initial approach of being relaxed and non - aggressive, it will help to relax the prospect from perhaps their initial tense state. This will help prevent their invisible barrier going up, which will most likely happen if you act too enthusiastic and unleash a whole load of spiel as soon as they first open their door. In other words, it will keep the prospect in a green or amber state rather than put them in a negative or red state.

Once you have introduced yourself, your next spoken words need to grab the prospect's attention. You can do that by saying something like, "I think we owe you an apology," which will capture the prospect's interest as they will be thinking, "apology for what?" Or you could say, "I was wondering if you could help?" This again will capture their interest as most people want to help if asked. You should then create a sense of loss, as described in Chapter 1, by saying, "it appears my colleague may have missed you out last week." "Missed me out for what?" they will be thinking. You then go on and explain what it is you have been doing for a lot of their neighbours in the area. This could be that you have been booking people in for surveys, or it could be that you have been offering some promotion, or it may be that you have been reducing people's utility bills. All you are doing is painting a picture that a lot of people are getting involved in the area with whatever it is you are doing, and that the prospect got missed out last week or whenever. You are not necessarily attempting to sell the prospect anything. Rather you are there to inform them what you have been doing for a lot of their neighbours, and it is up to them as to whether or not they get involved!

This approach will sound far less scripted/sales - like and will create far more interest as opposed to saying, "Hi how are you? My name is Andrew, and I'm from XYZ. The reason I am calling is that of blah, blah, blah." By using this bog standard approach, you will just sound like every other sales rep that has been around and as a result, you will most likely get a block straight away.

It is important at this stage to judge if the prospect is a complete waste of your time? Are they going to listen (and digest) what you have to say? Or are they just going to be rude and awkward to deal with? There is more on identifying different types of prospects in Chapter 2.

Once you have created interest in your opening line and have told them where you are from and what you are doing, you now need to qualify the prospect in order to save wasting your time. So you will need to know if they are the bill payer, whether or not they are in a contract with their existing provider, or whatever other qualifying questions you need to ask.

Now that you have created sufficient interest and have qualified the prospect, your next goal depending on what you are selling is to get inside their house. However, when I was booking people in for surveys for free solar panels, or when I was asking people to join a weekly lottery to support the charity, then doing the whole pitch on the doorstep was ok since it was a relatively straightforward affair.

A typical pitch I would do on the doorstep when doing the free solar would go something like:

Introduction…. Hi, I was wondering if you could help? I'm from XYX. I think we owe you an apology as I think my colleague may have missed you out last week. I don't know if you have already heard from some of your neighbours, or perhaps you may have seen some of our vans in the area over the past few days, but XYZ has been doing surveys on a number of properties in this area to find out who qualifies for free solar panels.

Presentation … Now we are not selling the panels. Rather we are putting our panels on houses that we think are suitable. The way it works, is we get paid for every unit of electricity produced via the Government Initiative, called the "Feed-in-Tariff," which is why it doesn't cost the homeowner anything. In return the homeowner will get to use whatever electricity is produced from the panels, meaning it will reduce their electricity bill by an average of 30 - 40%.

Close… Now I am not offering you the panels because you may not qualify, but like I said, I am booking people in for a survey, which we are doing over the next ten days for those that got missed out last time. I have about half a dozen slots left in the surveyor's diary, which I am filling in today. The survey takes about half an hour to do. They will have a quick look in your loft, and they will let you know approximately ten days later if you qualify. Assuming you do qualify, you can then decide for yourself if you want the panels. So shall I put you down for a survey like a lot of your neighbours?

With the charities, my pitch would go something like:

Introduction.... Hi, are you alright? It's just a quick call from XYZ. We are just asking people if they would be kind enough to support us by playing our weekly lottery.

Presentation .... Now I appreciate you may get a lot of charities asking for your support, but the reason why a lot of your neighbours say that they support us over other charities is because of XYZ. However, without the support of the public, we will be unable to continue doing the good work that we do, which I am sure you would agree would be a great shame, yeah?

Most of your neighbours are just playing a couple of lines a week, so it only costs £2.00 a week - less than the price of a cup of coffee! You can play for as little or as long as you like, and because it's a lottery, you have a chance of winning up to £1,000 on a weekly basis!

Close ... So can I put you down for a couple of lines like the rest of your neighbours?

As you can see from the above examples, the pitches are very simple and do not go into great depth. Notice in the solar pitch that I create interest in the opening line. I then briefly explain how the free solar works and how the customer benefits. I then create a certain amount of fear of loss by saying they need to qualify. And finally, I close them. Remember, your pitch is just a basic structure. You will not just read it out as it's written. Rather you will be more conversational and will also have some interaction from the prospect.

When pitching people, you should avoid asking yes/no questions - especially early on in your pitch because it's easy for a prospect to say, "no," meaning your pitch will come to an abrupt end. So I do not ask the prospect if I can show them how it works, nor do I ask them if they would like to save money. Instead, I am more assumptive and just continue with my presentation. Remember, the more presentations you do, the more sales you will make.

With the charity pitch, the format is slightly different since I am not providing a solution to a particular problem. Rather I am appealing to their good will. Therefore, I don't bother capturing their interest in the opening line as I would normally do. Also, because the charity was well known and respected for what it did, I didn't need to explain what the charity did. Rather I just needed to give them a reason to support us and tell them how the charity is different to others. If the charity isn't well known, then yes you need to explain a little about all the good work that the charity does and again give a good reason as to why they should donate. Perhaps it's a local charity, or perhaps it is a rescue charity that they may need themselves one day.

By saying that most of their neighbours already support us, it may make them feel more compelled to do the same as it will stir up an emotional feeling of guilt. Notice how I say that most people play just a couple of lines a week, so it only costs £2.00 a week. By pitching the higher amount, not only do you have room for manoeuvre, but it also means that you get double the commission! Therefore, if the prospect says they already donate to lots of other charities, then you can always drop down to only one line a week by saying, "yes I understand. A few of your neighbours also support other charities, so what they have done is rather than playing two lines they are just playing the one line for only £1:00 a week." Sure, if I could see that someone really didn't want to donate, or really couldn't afford it, then I didn't make them feel guilty. I just understood and moved on.

For those that agreed to play two lines, I would still need to give them the option to play only one line because if I didn't, they would be able to see for themselves from looking at the form that there was an option to play only one line. So as I was filling out the form, I would say, "like I said, most people are playing two lines a week, but there is a tiny percentage of people who are playing only one line. So shall I put you down for the two lines like most people, yeah?" Since I had already sold them on two lines, most people would just stick with that. Only a tiny percentage of people would drop to one line. Whereas if I was to pitch it in a different way by asking the prospect from the start if they want to play one line or two, most would say, "well just put me down for the one line for now."

When you have to do a fact find on the prospect's current situation and then match your presentation to their needs, then you do need to get inside their house because people do not digest the information at the door the same way as they would if you were sitting inside their house. An added advantage of going in and out of people's houses, is that neighbours across the street may see you going in and out of houses so will assume those people are getting involved even if they are not.

By going inside their house, you also have a better chance of speaking to their partner, if they have one, or to whoever else that might be inside the house. If you just talk to the one person on the door, and they then go back inside the house and tell their partner, the partner could very well just say they are not interested. That is because they don't understand what it is you are selling because the person who you spoke to at the door will be unable to sell the product as well as you can.

So when going into people's houses, I would still do a basic pitch on the door as shown above for the free solar and charities, but instead of closing them to make a decision, I would just close them to go inside their house instead. So with the gas and electric, the pitch will go something like:

Introduction... Hi, I was wondering if you could help? I am from XYZ and have been speaking to everyone in the area who is on a prepay meter who got missed out last week. Have you heard from any of your neighbours what we have been doing?

Presentation... Well, you are probably already aware that those on prepay meters pay more for their gas/electric than those on credit meters. But what I have found is about 80% of people who were on a prepay meter were paying a far higher rate than they need to. So all I have done for those that qualified was reduced the cost, meaning more money in people's pocket where it belongs. But like I said, you do need to qualify, which is why I am here.

Qualify... Now is it yourself who pays for your gas and electric? Do you have a standard prepay meter or a smart meter? And are you in receipt of any government help towards your energy?

Close ... Ok, well if I can just step inside for a minute and I'll show you what we are doing.

Whatever product you canvass, it is a good idea to try and create some level of dissatisfaction in your pitch and then provide the solution. So in the above example, I am creating dissatisfaction by saying people on prepay meters already pay more than those on credit meters and that 80% of people were paying more than they need to on their meter. And with subscription television, I would quite often create dissatisfaction by saying that people were receiving a bad signal through their standard aerial, or that there was not much to watch on their television apart from lots of repeats, etc.

However, when you create dissatisfaction, do not ask the prospect if they are experiencing the same problem because they will either not realise they have a problem or will not admit to having a problem. Instead, they will just say, "I'm fine. I haven't got a problem." Therefore, I just continue with my pitch by telling the prospect what I have been doing for everyone else before closing them to get inside their house. As you can see, I keep the presentation very brief. It is more of a summary rather than a presentation. I'll save the finer details for when I am inside their house.

When asking the closing question to get inside the prospect's house, you need to break eye contact and be pointing into the house as you step forward slightly. That will in most cases cause them to step back and let you in as you seem in control and are confident in what you are doing. You need to come across as if you have been inside everybody's house and that you just expect to go into theirs too!

Other ways you can get inside someone's house is to ask to look at something inside their house. So with the gas/electric, you can quite often get inside a prospect's house by asking to look at their electric meter, which is of interest because it will show how much they are paying for their electricity. And obviously, when doing the loft insulation, I had a perfect excuse to get inside their house as I needed to look inside their loft to measure their existing level of insulation. What you are asking to look at may not always be of interest to you, but it just acts as an excuse to get into people's houses. For example, when doing subscription television, I would ask to look at the back of their television for a "SCART" connection, and when I was doing phone and broadband, I would ask to look at their telephone socket, neither of which was of any real interest to me. You can even ask the prospect if they have a flat surface that you can lean on so that you can show them what you're doing. Mind you, on occasions when I did that, the prospect went back inside their house and came out with a tray or a book for me to lean on! Not exactly what I had in mind!

Once you are inside their house, you can give yourself a pat on the back as you are half way there to getting the sale. Not only will the prospect feel slightly more relaxed, but you will too! If they don't let you in, then you need to reassure them that it will only take a few minutes.

Now rather than go straight into your pitch, you should ask the prospect questions about something you have noticed in their house, or complement something in the house that you have noticed. For example, you could comment on a picture you have noticed, or if you see a musical instrument, you can ask them about that. What you are doing here is building a relationship with the prospect to build trust because like I said earlier on in the book: the more you take an interest in someone else, the more they will begin to like and trust you. Therefore, asking questions about themselves or admiring things in their house will create the relationship you need to help you get the sale. You don't need to get carried away with this. Just a couple of questions or a couple of compliments will be sufficient.

Once you have established a relationship with the prospect, you can now go to the second stage of your sales pitch: The **Fact Find**. Here you need to ask the prospect open-ended questions and listen to what they say so that you have an understanding of the prospect's current situation and how your product can improve their situation. Obviously, the fact find is relatively straight forward with the gas/electric in that all you need to know is who their current provider is, what tariff they are on, and how much they are currently spending.

But when switching people's phone and broadband service, or when selling subscription television, I would need to go into more detail before I was to present my product so that I could make sure that I put them on the right package. I would ask questions like, "so how often do you use your phone?" "Do you use your phone at any time of the day or just the evening and weekends?" "Do you think you would use your phone more if you had free calls in the day?" "Do you know anyone who lives abroad?" If so, do you ever call them?" "Would you call them more if all your calls were free?" "What do you usually use the internet for?" "Do you do a lot of downloading or is it just general browsing?" "How many computers do you have in the house?" "When you watch television, what type of things do you like to watch?" "Do you like comedies, documentaries, sports, movies, etc.?"

If you make the mistake of going straight into your presentation, then you run the risk that the features and benefits, which you think will be of interest to the prospect, are in fact of no interest at all to the prospect. For example, it would be no good me saying that you get free international calls all day seven days a week if you do not know anyone abroad. Similarly, it would be no good saying that you have an unlimited download limit on your broadband if you do not do much downloading. Likewise, when selling subscription television, it would be no good me saying that you can watch all the big sports matches if you have no interest in sports. Therefore, it is imperative that you find out about the prospect before you present anything, which is why it is so important that you listen carefully to what the prospect is telling you. After all, you would not go to a doctor's surgery and be immediately prescribed medicine without first having an examination of your current problem. If the doctor did that, he or she might well prescribe the wrong medication!

Once you have gathered all the relevant information, you need to get agreement from the prospect that you have accurately diagnosed their current situation before moving on to the third stage of the pitch: The **Presentation**. Here you will need to tailor your presentation to meet the requirements of the prospect.

When presenting, you must always remember to Keep It Short and Simple (KISS)! Going into too much depth will not only bore the prospect, but it will also confuse them too. You must also focus your presentation on what your product does rather than what it is because people do not buy the actual product: rather they buy the benefits that they perceive they will gain from using your product.

At every step of the presentation, you need to gain confirmation to make sure they are listening and that you are on the right track. For example, you would say, "so from now on you will have free calls abroad (feature), meaning you can call your sister in Australia whenever you feel like without worrying about the cost (benefit)! How would that make you feel? (close)"

You should go through each feature and benefit that is relevant (perhaps 3 or 4 features and benefits) and then gain that confirmation. This will widen the gap between where they currently are without your product to where they could be with your product. In other words, you are creating more and more dissatisfaction with their current situation while also creating more and more desire for your product. Think of the presentation like heating water on a stove. Once the water reaches 100 degrees, the water is at boiling point, or buying temperature, and every time you give a feature and benefit you are heating that water closer to buying temperature.

It is imperative that price does not come up until after you have fully explained the features and benefits of your product because it is important to build value in what you are doing before you offer the price. If you bring up the price too early, then the prospect could quite easily say they can't afford it since they do not see the value in what it is you are selling. If the prospect asks for the price early on in the presentation, you must divert their attention away from this issue without running the risk of making them lose their patience. You could say something like, "that's a good question, I'll come to that in a minute." If the prospect is insistent, then you could say something like, "I fully understand that you want to know how much it is going to cost. However, tell me something. Is the price the only thing that you will base your decision on?"

When you do deliver the price, it is a good idea to either water the price down or to break the price up to make it sound more affordable. When I was selling loft insulation, I would typically go into the prospect's loft and measure their existing level of insulation. I would then come down and show them on my tape measure what level of insulation they currently had and would show them what the current standards say the insulation should be. I would then explain that by only having the level of insulation they currently had a lot of heat from their house would be seeping through the ceiling and into the loft area, which in turn would exit the house. I would explain that by insulating their loft to the correct standard, it would stop the heat at the ceiling, meaning they would not need their heating on for as long and would therefore save money. I would then explain how we would insulate the entire loft to the correct standard and then carefully cut the edges to prevent condensation building up and that we would insulate the water tanks as well as draught proofing the loft hatch. Now that I had created sufficient value, I would then deliver the price and would water that price down. So I would say the cost of doing the job would be £400. I would then pause for a second or two so that the prospect would think that is what it was going to cost. I would then go on and explain the grant would pay for the majority of the cost, meaning it would only cost the prospect £169 to do the entire job. That is far more effective than simply going up the loft and telling them they need insulation and that it's going to cost £169 to do the job.

When selling subscription television, I would break the price down to a weekly amount and then show how insignificant that cost was. So for example, I would say, "a lot of your neighbours are getting these high-quality channels for as little as £5:00 per week, which is currently about the price of a portion of fish and chips or a couple of drinks down at the local pub." That was effective because most people would not think twice about buying a portion of fish and chips or a couple of drinks at the local pub.

Once you have delivered the price, you now need to go to the fourth stage of your pitch, which is the **CLOSE.** This should be relatively easy and straightforward providing you have followed the above steps correctly. By now the prospect should have reached buying temperature and will feel that going ahead with your product is just the obvious thing to do. They will feel as if they have made the decision for themselves rather than have been pushed into it. Remember: people like to buy, but they do not like to be sold to!

When I was selling subscription television, I would sometimes use an alternative close by saying something like, "a lot of your neighbours are getting installed on a weekday, but some prefer to get installed on a weekend. What would be best for you?" By asking this question, not only am I assumptive, but I am also asking the prospect to make a smaller decision, i.e. whether to get installed on the weekday or the weekend.

Another type of close I would quite often use was to explain the process of what was going to happen. For example, I would say something like, "well, all I need to do now is fill out the form, ring it through to the office to get an appointment date, and then you will get installed in approximately 2 - 3 weeks. Does that sound ok to you?" That would quite often work as the presentation was so good that going ahead with my product just seemed the natural thing to do.

And with the gas/electric you can say something like, "I take it you would prefer to have the extra money in your pocket rather than give it to your gas/electric company, yeah? Well, all that happens now is that we will contact your current energy provider, so you don't have to. We will then send you a new key and card within three weeks, just like we're doing for everyone else, and you can then top your meter up just like you do now at your local shop. So does that sound good to you?" And if the prospect is a little hesitant and says," Umm," you can just help them slightly with their decision by saying something like, "well you might as well. The money is better off in your pocket than theirs (referring to their current gas/electric company)." Quite often this will be all that it takes just to push them over the edge.

Once you have closed the prospect and turned any objections, you should immediately get your form out and begin filling it in. You must not mess about or go through anything else at this stage because it's still fairly delicate, and if you're not careful, you could easily lose the prospect. Only until after you have gone through your final stage of the pitch: the **CONSOLIDA-TION,** can you relax a little bit. The purpose of the consolidation is to make sure the sale stays in bed. It is no good if all the hard work you have put in to get the sale only cancels after a couple of days or so once the initial impulse wears off and buyer's remorse sets in. Remember, you have not earned your commission just by signing them up. It's not until it has been installed or gone past the cooling off period that you have actually earned your money.

To minimise the amount of cancellations you get (you can never completely avoid them), firstly, make sure that you put the prospect on a package that they can realistically afford. It is no good putting them on something that is above their budget as a customer will most likely phone up the company to cancel rather than reduce their package.

Secondly, you need to write everything down. You need to write down the process of what is going to happen next, and if their first bill is going to be higher, due to having to pay a month in advance, then you need to explain this clearly so that the customer has no nasty surprises. Once you have explained everything to the customer, you should ask them if they have any questions just in case you have missed something.

And finally, you need to pre-empt any possible negatives that your prospect may hear because once a prospect has made a buying decision, they will naturally want to justify that decision by talking to others. This could be other family members, friends, or even work colleagues. Now this can be a real danger if you are not careful. It will only take a tiny negative comment to destroy your sale. That used to be a real problem when doing free solar due to the many myths that were flying about regarding the free solar industry. The common myths were that you had problems when you came to sell your house, and if you needed repairs to your roof, then the company would charge you to remove the panels. Now this was the case with some companies offering free solar, but not the company to which I was representing. Never- the-less, people would assume we were the same, and as a result, they would sometimes cancel on me if I failed to address those myths.

I remember one time I called a customer who cancelled on me. She told me that the reason she decided to cancel was that some friends of hers told her that the solar panels would not generate enough power in the daylight, meaning she would have to be careful how she used her electricity or else she would be without power. Then in the evening, when it's dark, and the panels stop producing electricity, she would be charged a higher rate for her electricity as a result of having solar panels. Now that was complete nonsense, yet my customer believed what her friends had told her as absolute fact. Unfortunately, once she had made her mind up, there was no way that I was going to be able to turn her around.

Another customer who rang me up to cancel told me that she had been speaking to her neighbour Janet and that Janet told her that the company owns your roof and that you don't get any of the electric produced. Rather the company who puts the panels on your roof gets all the electricity! Again this was complete garbage. Luckily, however, I managed to turn her around. Firstly, I agreed to cancel the survey since she did not wish to proceed. That was to prevent her from getting all defensive. I then explained that although her neighbour thought she knew all about our company, in actual fact, she didn't. I explained the facts to the customer and reassured her that her neighbour was talking a load of nonsense.

It is very unfortunate, but as these two examples clearly show: ignorance does not lead to silence! You must remember that at all times. Many people like to think they know it all and that they are the experts when in reality they know absolutely nothing about your company or the product you are selling. They are negative people who actively search for anything negative to say about your company, regardless of whether it's true or not.

Therefore, to minimise other people destroying your sale, make sure that you pre - empt any possible negatives that people are going to hear. You need to be up front, and you must not shy away from anything, because if you do, you will pay the price!

CHAPTER 7
OVERCOMING BLOCKS/ OBJECTIONS

There is a world of difference between turning a negative that a prospect may throw at you and attempting to turn a negative/rude person around. The former you can do with a little practice, but the latter you are wasting your time. It is simply not worth the time and effort to try and turn a negative/rude person around. They may well have spent their whole adult life being negative, so what chance have you got when you are only spending a few minutes with them?

You can deal with objections either before they are brought up, known as pre-empting objections, or after they have been brought up. The idea of pre-empting objections is that you are taking the steam away from the objection, and you are not afraid to hide from it. You are confident in dealing with it head on. If you fail to deal with objections in this way, then a prospect may reject your offer without actually telling you as to why they are not interested. Instead, they will keep that issue to themselves, yet you will be puzzled as to why they don't want to go ahead. For example, when doing free solar, I knew a lot of people would be thinking to themselves that you don't get anything for free and that there must be a catch. So instead of ignoring this, I told them myself that you don't normally get anything for free and that there is usually a catch. I then went on to explain the reason as to why it was free. Also, when switching people's phone and broadband service, or their gas/electric, quite often people would be concerned that the price would go up six months down the line. So rather than ignore this, I would confront it head on. I would explain that quite often companies would offer a low introductory price for you to join and then six months down the line they would put their prices up. I would then explain how we were different in that we offered a fixed tariff.

You will find that you will always get the same blocks and objections, so you will soon be able to learn how to deal effectively with them. There are common objections such as, "I am happy as I am," or "I need to think about it" as well as product-specific objections such as, "I do not want a satellite dish," or "the cavity is there for a reason so should not be filled with insulation." What's important, is that you don't buy into any negatives. For example, when I was doing the free solar, I once had an estate agent tell me that you cannot sell your house with free solar panels installed due to it being a 25-year lease. However, I had a photograph on my phone that showed a house with our solar panels on and it had a sold sign outside the house. When I showed the estate agent this, he admitted to the fact that he worked for the same estate agency selling the house. However, it would have been all too easy for me to have bought into this negative.

You must also make sure that you never over- react to what a prospect says. You need to play the game smarter! So if a prospect is getting all excited and saying they're happy as they are, or they are not changing, etc. it's best that you remain calm and allow them to get it all off their chest. Do not attempt to battle with them or correct them in any way. Just be agreeable so that you calm them down and bring them into a more "amber state."

You also need to be aware that an objection that a prospect gives you is not always the real objection: it is merely a smokescreen. For example, a prospect may tell you they need to think about it, or that they are happy as they are when in reality it is because they don't buy at the door, or don't trust you but do not want to tell you this. That is why is it imperative that you focus your attention on building a relationship with the prospect. By doing this, you will receive far fewer objections and will therefore make more sales.

Finally, there is no foolproof way to deal with objections. It is still essentially a numbers game. You simply will not be able to turn everyone around. It is just not possible. But if ten people were to give you a particular objection, rather than lose all ten people, you may be able to turn four or five people around, and as a result, you will increase the number of sales that you do.

Below is a list of the most common blocks/objections that you will hear and an explanation of how to effectively deal with them. If you get **2 or 3 No's** of the same objection, then you should just walk away rather than waste your time.

I Am Not Interested!

This is the most common block that you will hear. However, it is nothing more than just a natural reaction that people have to someone who comes to their door trying to sell something.

In order to minimise hearing this block, you need to come across as different to the stereotypical salesperson. Therefore, you must be relaxed and indifferent and create as much interest in your opening line as possible as described in Chapter 6. You can also use distraction techniques if you can see that the prospect is going to tell you they are not interested. So for example, if you can see from the prospect's body language that they are just about to say they are not interested, you can distract them and take them away from their current train of thought. You can do this by interrupting them and asking them in a confused tone of voice something like, "sorry is this number 44?" Or "sorry, have I got the right house? Is this number 44 St. David's Close?" You would then continue with your pitch as normal.

If you still get people saying that they are not interested - despite acting relaxed and indifferent on the door, then you need to firstly deflect the block, then capture their interest, and then fire a question at them. That way they will forget about what they had initially said, i.e., they're not interested, but instead, they will focus on answering the question. So when someone says, "I'm not interested," you could say, "that's fine. It's not about that. I've just had a few complaints from some of your neighbours about their prepay meters; that's all. Have you still got a prepay meter?" You would then go on and tell them how people were complaining that they were paying too much for their gas and electric. Alternatively, you could just say, "that's fine. It's not about that. I owe you an apology. We missed you out last week; that's all. Have any of your neighbours told you what we have been doing?" Someone who I used to work with replied by saying, "nor am I" when someone said that they were not interested and then immediately fired a question at them. Like I said above, in a lot of cases this will focus the prospect's mind away from being not interested and will instead focus their mind on answering the question.

Once you have turned the block, it is important that you don't allow it to affect you in any way. You must forget what they said and continue your pitch as normal. If you don't, you will find yourself rushing through your pitch and not putting as much effort into it as you will be thinking in the back of your mind that they're not really interested anyway.

If you do get past the initial introduction, and the prospect now knows what you are doing, they may still say they are not interested. If they do, then I find that the best way to deal with this is to pretend to accept it. The prospect has most likely misunderstood what it is you are doing and has jumped to conclusions. That was quite often the case when I was doing the free solar because they thought I was selling them (despite me saying they were free). It was also a problem when I was doing subscription television because they thought it was going to cost them a lot of money and that it was only good if you like sports, etc. What you need to understand is that the prospect simply does not have enough information available at this point to make an intelligent decision. They are ignorant of the facts, but unfortunately, they are ignorant of their own ignorance and as a result will shut themselves off. This can be a bit of a dilemma because you cannot avoid telling them where you are from just because you are fearful that they will shut themselves off. Therefore, what you have to do is learn how to deal effectively with this type of block. In fact, you are doing people a big favour by turning this block as you are not forcing someone to have something they neither need nor want. Rather you just want them to make an intelligent decision that may benefit them. But without knowing what you are doing, how in reality can they make an intelligent decision?

By pretending to accept what they are saying, you will calm the prospect down and get them into a more "amber state." So you need to say something like, "ok no problem, I'll cross you off my list as it's not for everyone." They may still say they are not interested because they are expecting you to try and argue with them or persuade them to listen to you. You then again say the same thing: "no that's not a problem. It's not a problem at all. I'll cross you off my list. Like I said, it's not for everyone." You then put your brochure/pitch card back in your folder and turn to walk away. You then ask, "just out of curiosity, is there any particular reason as to why you are not interested?" At this point, their guard will be lowered as you have accepted that they are not interested and have turned to walk away. The prospect may now tell you as to why they are not interested. If they do, then you can deal with that objection in a very gentle way so as not to put them back into the red state again.

Once they have given you the objection, it is important that you agree and not try to correct them. So when doing the free solar, I would quite often hear people say, "well I've looked into solar panels, and they are not worth it at my time of life." So instead of correcting them, as they thought I was selling them, I simply agreed and said, "yes I agree with you. You have obviously looked into it in depth and know a lot about it (stroking ego)." I would then bring in a third party story by saying something like, "In fact, I've just been speaking to a gentleman down the road, and he said the same thing. Just like you, he is very knowledgeable and has decided it's not worth buying solar panels at his time of life. However, the reason he has decided to get involved today is that they are not going to cost him anything, but instead, they are going to reduce his electric bill significantly." I would then explain as to why the panels were not going to cost him anything. I have gained many sales from using this approach, and you can gain an enormous amount of satisfaction from someone who initially says that they are not interested, to 5 minutes later when they have agreed to go ahead!

If, on the other hand, the prospect does not give you an actual reason as to why he/she is not interested and just says, "I'm just not interested," then there is not a lot you can do. Perhaps they don't trust you, or maybe they don't deal with anyone at the door but are just not telling you this. Whatever their reason, forget them and move on. Time is money!

I Am Busy!

This block is quite often another way to get rid of you. You can sometimes tell as to whether or not someone is genuinely busy. If they look rushed off their feet, or they have kids screaming, then obviously they are busy, so you should just apologise and tell them you will try and catch them another time. Under no circumstances attempt to pitch them as they will be unable to digest fully what it is you are saying. As a result, they will probably reject your offer, or if they do agree to go ahead, they will most likely cancel on you since they don't fully understand what it is that they have agreed to.

The same rules apply to prospects who are on the phone (or pretending to be). Quite often they will ask you what it is about, but you must not tell them because if you do say what you are doing, then they are most likely to tell you they are not interested just so that they can get rid of you. Far better to apologise and say that it's nothing serious, but you will try and catch them another time. You then just turn around and walk off.

If on the other hand someone says they are busy, but you see no obvious signs that they are busy, then there is a good chance they are only trying to get rid of you. In these circumstances you would simply say, "yes tell me about it, so am I. I'll only take a minute since you are busy." You would then carry on with your pitch as normal.

Are You Selling Something?

When you get this block, you must not answer the question. If you say, "yes," then the sale will be lost, and if you say, "no," then you will be lying because you might be selling them something. Besides, they won't believe you anyway. Therefore, it is best if you do not answer their question, but instead, you distract them by capturing their interest. So you say, "well actually I think I owe you an apology." You then go on and explain that your colleague missed them out last week, etc. It is much the same way how politicians avoid awkward questions: they do not directly answer the question!

Is This About Switching?

When someone immediately asks you if it's about switching, then you know full well that if you say, "yes," the prospect will just tell you that they are not interested and will most likely shut themselves off since they don't yet realise the benefits of switching. And once a prospect has shut themselves off, it can be extremely difficult to get them to listen to you. However, you can't say, "no" because you might end up switching them. So instead, you should first of all try and ignore their question - just like you do when they ask you if you're selling something. You should then capture their interest, and then fire a question or a series of questions at them. So after they have asked you if it's about switching, you say, "well actually I've been speaking to a lot of your neighbours about their meters, and a lot of them have been paying more than they need to. Is it yourself who pays for your gas/electric?" If they ask you again if it's about switching, then you should deflect the block, capture their interest, and then again immediately fire a question or a series of questions at them. So you could say, "well no, not if you don't benefit. Do you have a pre-pay meter for your gas as well as for your electric?" By doing this, it should allow you to regain control of the conversation. Remember, you are not there to force the prospect to have something they don't want. Rather, you just want them to listen to what you have to say before either accepting or rejecting your offer.

I'm Happy as I am!

This can be either a block or an objection. If someone immediately says to you "I am happy as I am," then this is just an attempt to block the sales conversation. Therefore, you should just agree, then capture their interest, and then fire a question. So you respond by saying, "that's good to hear! In fact, everyone is happy with the level of service they are receiving. It's not about that, though. I've just had a lot of complaints; that's all. Unfortunately, I've found approximately 80% of your neighbours were paying more than they need to for their gas/electric. Now is it yourself who pays for your gas/electric? And do you have a pre-pay meter for both your gas and for your electric?"

If they tell you again that they are happy, then they are simply in defence mode. There is no way that you will get a prospect to listen to you when they are in that mode. No matter what you say, they will keep saying they are "happy as they are." Therefore, you need to neutralise them in much the same way as when they tell you they're not interested. So you accept that they are happy and turn to walk away. You then ask, "just out of curiosity…may I ask what it is you are happy about?" The prospect will now say something like, "well, I'm just happy with the level of service I am receiving." You then say, "well, I am glad to hear it. In fact, most people who I have been speaking to today also said they were happy with the level of service they were receiving. However, we are not here to change that. What we are doing is XYZ, which is the reason why everyone has decided to get involved" At least now the prospect may listen to you, so you have a chance of selling to them!

If, however, you get people saying they are happy as they are after you have presented your product, then this is an objection. You must remember that people do not like change. Familiarity is what breeds safety. Stepping into the unknown can make people feel anxious. Therefore, you need to present your product as an improvement over what they already have since most people are open to improving their life in one way or another.

When I was selling phone and broadband service, many people would use this objection as they had perhaps been with their current provider for many years and were quite happy with the level of service they were receiving. Therefore, they would take the attitude: if it's not broke, why fix it?

It was important for the prospect to understand that by changing provider it was not some drastic change. They would still be able to use their telephone in the same way; their number would quite often stay the same; their internet would work in the same way; and if there were a problem with their phone line, the same people would come out and fix it. The only real difference is that they would be getting far better value for their money.

I Need to Speak to My Partner or Son/Daughter

With this objection, you need to know who the decision maker is so that you can arrange to call back either the same day or another day to speak to the decision maker. If, however, the prospect is the decision maker, or perhaps a joint decision maker, but still wants to ask their partner, then you should try and turn the objection. Sure, it's ideal that you speak to both decision makers, but if you don't turn the objection while you can, then you may never get a chance again. The next time you call on them, the prospect might not answer the door, or they may have told their partner that you had been around, and their partner could just say they are not interested since they don't fully understand your offer. Therefore, try and turn the objection while you can – especially if your product is going to save them money, and you are not going to be back in the area. So when someone tells you they need to ask their partner, you could say something like, "yes I can understand. That is what a lot of people have said to me today. However, once they realised that it was going to save them money rather than cost them, they felt no need to ask their partner. Now obviously I do not know your partner, but if they could save money on their electric bill, I am sure they would be happy, yeah? Well, why don't we book you in like everyone else and I'll leave you with all the details to show to your partner?"

If you do succeed in turning this objection, then make sure you write everything down on the leave behind material so that the other partner can read it when they get back. Remember, you can't rely on the person who you have spoken to, to be able to explain it to their partner as you have done to them.

If the partner happens to arrive back when you are still on the door, then you need to greet the partner immediately. This person is now the most important to you, and if you are not careful, they could easily destroy your sale. You will need to explain it all again so that the partner fully understands. If you make the mistake of ignoring the partner, then the partner could easily blow your sale, which has happened to me on occasions.

I Need to Think About It.

This is probably the most dreaded objection that any salesperson can hear. You have just gone through your sales presentation, highlighting all the features and benefits, and then at the end of your presentation, you get the prospect saying that they need to "think about it." "Think about what?" You will be thinking. "What on earth is there to think about?" But you do need to understand that from the prospect's point of view they have to put their trust in you and as the salesperson knocking their door, they will always hold a degree of scepticism towards you. Just because you say it will benefit them doesn't necessarily mean it will! After all, you might just say anything to get a sale!

This objection can mean one of two things: firstly, it could simply be the prospect's polite way of saying, "no." They do not want to upset you and therefore find it difficult to tell you that they are not interested. So instead, they say they need to think about it, which is, of course, giving you false hope. You will be able to recognise if this is the case by the way that they say it and through their body language. If they just come out and say, "I'll think about it," then they are not interested. Or if they are not really looking very interested, then again they are not interested, so forget them.

On the other hand, a prospect may be genuinely interested in your offer, but they are afraid of making a mistake. In fact, I would say nine times out of ten this will be the real reason – especially if you have presented your product correctly. Or perhaps they are unsure about a couple of things. Perhaps they are 90% there, but they just need that final push over the edge. Sometimes all you need to do is just go through the presentation again with them, or better still, relate to them a little bit more to build up more trust before closing them again.

If they still say they want to think about it, then you need to try and unearth what it is that is preventing them from going ahead. I find the best way to do this, is to show empathy. Avoid just coming out and saying, "what do you need to think about?" because it is too much to the point and can come across slightly aggressive and pushy.

Therefore, the best way to deal with this objection is to agree with the prospect. That will help to relax them so that they may reveal what they need to think about. You could say something like, "yes that's not a problem, but may I ask what it is you need to think about? Now if they tell you, then great, but if they don't, then you need to make suggestions. You could say something like, "a few of your neighbours said they needed to think about it, but the reason they needed to think about it was due to a few things that they were unsure about. Some were worried the price may go up in a few months' time. Others were just unsure about the process. Just out of curiosity, may I ask you what it is you are uncertain about? Is it the price? Or are you unsure as to the process?" Now hopefully they will reveal what it is they need to think about.

If you can fear of loss the prospect in some way, as explained in Chapter 1, then this will sometimes work. It all depends on what you are canvassing. For example, when switching people's gas/electric, it can be hard to fear of loss them because they know they can change anytime they like, and you are not offering any special incentives. But when booking people in for surveys for free solar, you could easily fear of loss them by saying you only have so many slots left in the surveyor's diary and that you won't be back in the area for another 18 months or so.

If you can't fear of loss people, and they still insist on "thinking about it," then the best is to say, "ok well that's not a problem. How long do you think you might need to think about it?" If they say, "well I'll need a few days," then just say, "well I am in the area for the next couple of days, so if I have time I'll give you a call after you have had a chance to think it over." Unfortunately, most people do not think it over, and even if they do they will just think of all the reasons why not to get involved, so I wouldn't make any special effort in going back. In fact, you can almost guarantee that when you do go back, the prospect will either say, "Oh I haven't had a chance yet to look into it," or they will say, "no I think I'll leave it for now." Just accept that you cannot sign up everyone as some people are simply too sceptical or too nervous to make any buying decision.

Can You Leave Me A Leaflet/Business Card?

If the prospect interrupts you mid - pitch and asks you to leave a leaflet, then what they are saying is that they are either busy or just not interested, in which case you should just ask them if they are busy and tell them you will give them a call later.

If a prospect asks you for a leaflet after you have given a presentation, then they may be interested in your offer, but they just need more reassurance before they commit. I find the best way to deal with this, is to say something like, "I would leave you with a leaflet, but unfortunately I don't have many left, so I can only leave leaflets with people who are getting involved. What is it you are unsure about?" You then just briefly summarise what you are doing again and relate to them a little more before closing them again.

If the prospect will just not commit and does not give a reason as to what's on their mind, then you should just forget them. Don't bother to leave a leaflet as left to their own devices people tend to either not give it a second thought once you've left their house, or if they do, they tend to think negative and think of all the reasons as to why not to get involved. And besides, you're not a post man!

I Can't Afford It.

This could be true in that the prospect may genuinely not have the money to purchase your product, or it could be that they don't see the value in your product. To minimise hearing this objection, you must always deliver the price **after** you have built sufficient value in your product. If, however, you still hear them say that they can't afford it, then ask them if they would take your product if it were free. If they say, "yes," then ask them why. This will make them reveal their buying motive. You can then ask them how much "too much" is. You can then work with the difference between what they are prepared to pay and what the product costs rather than having to work with the total cost. You would then build more value and show the prospect why the extra amount is money well spent.

I Do Not Buy at The Door!

This type of prospect is probably going to be a waste of time. Therefore, I wouldn't spend much time with them. The best thing to do here is just to say something like, "that's ok. I'm just letting you know what I am doing for others in the area, that's all." If they want to get involved too, then great! If not, then that's up to them. Don't worry about it! Who cares?

CHAPTER 8
TEN DEADLY SINS

Below are what I think are the ten deadliest sins that you should never commit while in the field.

1. Never Argue

You must never argue with a prospect - even if you know you are right and what they are saying is 100% wrong. Therefore, it is important that you always agree with the prospect, and only when they have sufficiently calmed down and got everything off their chest can you gently correct them. Remember: you are there to win a sale and not an argument!

2. Never Be Rude

You are calling on prospects without being invited to do so. You are on their premises at a time that may be inconvenient. Although it is sometimes tempting to be rude back and give some sarcastic remark - especially when you have had a tough day, you must under no circumstances bring yourself down to that level. Remember, you are a professional sales person, so you must at all times act in a professional way. You have to bear in mind that they may well know a lot of people in the area, and if you offend them, they could let everyone know, and some may even be people who you have managed to sign up and may now cancel. It means when a prospect says, "I am not interested," you do not say what you might feel like saying, such as: "so you're not interested in saving money then?" Or "well if you took the time to listen instead of being so damn ignorant, then you might learn something!" It is not professional for you to do so, so you must bite your tongue and move on!

3. Never Be Pushy

Nobody likes a pushy salesperson. Even if you do manage to sign them up, they will most likely cancel on you anyway. I appreciate that it can be frustrating when a prospect does not want to go ahead - despite you knowing full well that the product or service would benefit them because as a result, you both lose! But you should never have to try too hard to get someone to say, "yes." So if you get the same objection 2 - 3 times, then it's best just to move on.

4. Never Get Emotionally Involved

Dealing with people can be a real pain in the ass! Some will be rude; some will say they need to "think about it," even when making the most minor of decisions; and some will reject your offer without knowing anything about it. But what you must not do is allow yourself to get emotionally involved. Sure, you're human, and yes, at times perhaps you will allow yourself to get emotionally involved, but you do need to snap out of it as quickly as you can. Take a break, or if you are in a terrible state, then go home! There is no point in knocking doors if you are not in the right mental state. You will be a walking time bomb waiting to go off! All you need now is some awkward or rude prospect to slam the door in your face!

You must also never take anything anyone says or does personally. They do not know you well enough to make any form of judgement about you, other than they do not like you knocking on their door. Just move on and accept it as part of the job.

5. Never Knock the Competition

It is ok for the prospect to knock the competition, but you must never do so. If you do, then you look unprofessional and run the risk of the prospect getting defensive - especially if they have your competitor's product! The best thing to say is, "I cannot comment on the level of service they give as I have never had their service. However, a few people in the area have told me that the broadband speed can at times be a bit slow or if you have a problem it's impossible to get to speak to someone." Now the prospect cannot get defensive with me because it is not me saying this, rather it is some of their neighbours in the area who are telling me this. The great thing about this is that you can bring about a certain amount of dissatisfaction with their current product without you attacking the other company.

6. Never Tell Malicious Lies

You are a professional sales person who has a product to sell. By telling malicious lies you not only discredit your company, but you also discredit your profession as a salesperson. So do not make claims about your product that are untrue. Telling white lies about all their neighbours getting involved, or telling them you only have so many left, are lies that help people make buying decisions. They are not lies that will cause the prospect financial loss, etc. After all, if you were to tell the truth when someone was to ask you if anybody else got involved, you might end up saying something like, "well the first person shut the door in my face, the second person was not interested, the third person hated the look of solar panels, the fourth person told me you don't get anything for free," and so on. However, none of these people have made intelligent decisions, so why should someone rely on the decisions of those people over their own?

7. Never Knock Doors If Customer Is Watching

When you sign up a customer, it is a good idea that you don't immediately knock their neighbours' doors if they are watching out of their window or are standing outside their house. If you do and their neighbours are rude to you or criticise your company, it will not look good – especially since you have been creating the picture that a lot of people in the area have been getting involved. It is best that you leave the doors until later on or come back another day.

8. Never Credit People with Making Intelligent Decisions

Once you have done door to door sales for a while, you will come to the conclusion that a large proportion of people do not make intelligent decisions. They will quite often reject your offer without knowing anything about it, and will believe myths told by friends as if they are concrete facts and will not try and uncover the facts for themselves. If you do credit the decisions made by people as intelligent decisions, it will only drive you crazy! You will find that you will be asking yourself questions like: "what's wrong with this person? Do they not understand? Have I done something wrong?" Just accept that they are decisions based on emotions and not rational well thought out decisions. Once you do that, you will find the job becomes a lot easier!

9. Never Rely On a Prospect to Sell Your Product to Their Partner

Prospects can be useless sales people. You can give a prospect an excellent presentation and then when the prospect explains what you have said to their partner, they just ask them if they are interested. They do not highlight all the features and benefits, and they do not use any of the tools as described in Chapter 1. Therefore, if possible, it is always a good idea if you can speak to the partner yourself, or if you can't, you need to write everything down – including all the features and benefits so that the partner can read what you have written down.

10. Never Make a Special Effort or Go Out of Your Way to Go to an Appointment

Appointments are quite often disappointments! A prospect can seem very interested when you see them for the first time. In fact, you could almost bet your life that they will go ahead, but when you go back, they either don't answer the door or say they have thought about it, but they have decided not to bother. So yes, by all means, go back to appointments but only when you happen to be in the area again.

CHAPTER 9
A DAY IN THE LIFE OF A CANVASSER

From what this book has taught you, I am now going to put it all together by giving you an example of a typical day pitching free solar and turning objections dealing with a variety of different prospects. I have also highlighted the downside of doing your whole pitch on the door, which although it will mean you can move around more quickly, it will inevitably lose some sales too.

Start time 14:30.

First five doors, no answer.

The next door I go to a young girl, aged about 21, answers the door. I immediately qualify her by asking her if she is the lady of the house. She informs me that she isn't and tells me her parents are away on holiday and won't be back until next week. Since I won't be in the area next week, I just cross the house off my list and move on.

The next door that I knock, the prospect immediately asks me what I am selling. I do not answer. Instead, I create interest by telling him we missed him out last week. I then go on and say, "I don't know if you have already heard from some of your neighbours, but we are doing the surveys in this area over the next two weeks." He replies: "surveys for what?" I explain that it is to see which houses qualify to get the free solar panels. "No I've looked into that before," he says. "I'm not interested! Not worth it at my time of life!" Obviously, the word free has not registered with him, and the door shuts before I have a chance to put him right!

I forget about him and move on to the next door. A lady answers. I use my same opening line, but she informs me she is only a tenant. I ask her if she speaks to her landlord often. She tells me that she doesn't as it's all through an agent. I decide to move on because it's not worth the hassle of trying to get in touch with the landlord through the agent.

The next door that I knock, a woman answers the door. I explain what I am doing, and she agrees to a survey. I tell her that the office will give her a ring within the next half an hour to give her an appointment date.

I knock eight more doors but no answer. On the eighth door, I can even see a person sitting in the lounge watching the television. I know he has heard the doorbell since it's quite loud, but he has apparently chosen to ignore it.

The next door I knock, a man answers, and before I can utter a word, he says, "whatever it is, I'm not interested!" and then shuts the door in my face!

The next door I go to, the person answers and points to their sticker on their window, which says they do not buy or sell at the door. The door shuts before I have a chance to say anything.

I knock three more doors but no answer.

I knock another door and speak to an elderly lady on a Zimmer frame. I tell her where I am from and explain that I am booking people in for surveys for free solar panels. I ask her if she is interested, knowing full well she will say, "no." I do not wish to book her in for a survey as she is too vulnerable. If she said she was interested, I would have left her a leaflet to give to her family.

I move on and knock another door. I speak to a middle - aged woman who tells me that her husband deals with everything and won't be back until 17:30. I make a note and move on.

I now get a call from the office informing me that the lady who agreed to a survey earlier on is not answering her phone. I decide to go back to her house to see what the problem is, but she does not answer the door. Unfortunately, until the office has given her a date, I have no booking, meaning no commission. But because she doesn't answer, I decide to move on. Perhaps I'll give her a ring later or call back another day, but for now, I can't afford to waste any time.

The next door I knock a gentleman answers. He agrees to a survey, so I phone it through to the office to get it booked on. The office then checks the house on Google Earth for any issues before they will book it in. However, they knock the house back due to shading from the flats opposite. I do not agree with this decision, but for now I have to accept it and move on. Perhaps I can get my manager to double check it for me and book it on another day.

The next ten doors I knock, there is no answer.

The next house that I go to, I can see that a man is washing his car, so I do not bother talking to him as he is clearly busy. I make a note of the house number and will call back later. I also miss out the next house because I don't want the person outside washing his car hearing the conversation I have with his neighbour just in case he/she is either rude or criticises my company.

The next door that I knock, a man in his mid - late 60's answers the door. I use my usual pitch. I apologise and ask him if he can help. I explain my colleague was in the area last week, but it appears he missed him out. I tell the man that we are doing the surveys to see which houses qualify for free solar panels. However, as soon as I mention the word: solar panels, he immediately tells me that he is not interested and puts his hand out in front of him. I accept what he says. I say, "ok that's not a problem." Again he says he is not interested, so again I tell him it's not a problem and that it's not for everyone. I tell him we will cross him off our list, and then I go to walk away. The prospect, looking a little bewildered, now lowers his guard. There is no need for him to be defensive. The threat has passed. As I begin to walk away, I ask, "just out of curiosity, is there any particular reason as to why you are not interested?" He tells me that he has looked into solar panels before, and they are not financially viable at his time of life. He has obviously got the wrong end of the stick, and the word free has not registered with him. Rather than correct him, which will only raise his guard again, I agree: "Yes I agree with you. It is certainly not worth you buying the solar panels. You have obviously looked into it and know your stuff (stroking his ego). In fact, I've just been speaking to someone down the road, and he said the same thing. He is about the same age as yourself and he also knows a lot about solar panels. However, the reason he has got involved (third party story), was because we are not selling the panels. What we are doing is putting our panels on what we think are suitable roofs. You as the homeowner will benefit from as much of the free electricity that the panels produce, meaning from now on a lot of your daylight electricity will be free. Therefore, if for example, you were to put your washing machine on in the day, it will be powered by the solar panels. Where we make our money from is that we get paid from the Government Initiative, the Feed-in-Tariff for having the panels on your roof generating renewable energy. Now all I am doing today is not offering you the panels since your roof may not be suitable (fear of loss), but I am booking people in for a free, no obligation survey to see if their roof qualifies." I then go on and explain that he is just one of many people in the area having a survey (imprinting) to see if they qualify while at the same time pointing at my list of names and addresses (sheep factor). I explain that we only come around every 18 months, and this may well be the last time that we come around (fear of loss). I then close the sale before I talk myself out of it. The prospect agrees, so I take his details down before writing on the leaflet that it's a free no obligation survey to see if his roof qualifies for free solar. I write down that the survey will take approximately 30 minutes and that we will let him know if suitable approximately two weeks later. By writing this down, it helps him to explain to his partner that it's only a survey, and secondly, it shows that they will be under no pressure to sign up on the day of the survey as we will let them know two weeks later - not on the day of the survey. I tell the prospect to listen out for his phone as he will receive a call within the next 30 minutes or so from the office to give him an appointment time.

It is now 16:30. I have been knocking doors for two hours and now, providing the prospect answers his phone, I have my first booking of the day!

I go to the next house. A woman answers the door. I explain to her that I have just been speaking to her next-door neighbour John (name dropping), and I tell her what we are doing for people in the area. She tells me that she is moving house shortly, which could be true, but it could be a lie. Either way, I move on.

I knock six more doors but no answer. The last house even had a long driveway, which I walked up for nothing.

The next door that I knock, I get a cold reception. The man stares at me with killer eyes. He looks at me as the enemy! I ask him how he is, but I get no reply - just a stare. I ask him again, but he angrily snaps: "Come on! What is it you want? Hurry up!" I think to myself that this is most certainly not a customer. It is not worth me spending any time with this person, so I brush him off by saying, "sorry are you busy?" He snaps: "yes!" I tell him I'll leave him to it, and without telling him where I am from or why I am there, I walk off. I will save my breath for the next house and gain a sense of satisfaction by walking away.

The next house that I knock, a friendly lady answers with her dog by her side. I ask what the dog's name is (relationship building). I tell her that I have a dog and what type of dog I have. I then explain why I am there. She tells me that she cannot stand the look of solar panels. I tell her that the solar panels are funded through a Government initiative so won't cost her anything, but they will save her a lot of money on her electric bill. She tells me that she doesn't care and that she would rather pay more for her electric than have the panels stuck on the front of her roof. I respect her decision and move on.

I knock a few more doors but all with no answer. It is now just gone 17:00, so I decide to take half an hour break.

At 17:30, I begin knocking the doors that I knocked earlier in the day where there was no answer. A man answers and informs me that he is eating his dinner. I apologise and tell him I'll perhaps catch him another time. I do not say what I am doing. He asks, but as I walk away, I turn around and say, "it's nothing serious, but I think my colleague missed you out last week, that's all. I'll catch you another time." I now make a note and will knock this door again on Saturday or perhaps later in the evening if I have time.

The next door I go to, a woman answers but says she is busy. I smell her dinner cooking, so I apologise and tell her I'll catch her another time. Again I do not say why I am there.

The next two houses are in darkness, so I save time and do not knock these doors.

The next door I go to, a man comes to the door and immediately asks me what I am selling. I do not answer. Instead, I say, "well actually I think we owe you an apology. I don't know if you have already heard from some of your neighbours living in the area, or if you have seen our van on the street over the past few days, but XYZ is doing surveys in this area to find out who qualifies for free solar panels." He says, "there is no such thing as a free lunch!" I do not try and correct him. Instead, I agree: "Yes that's right. You don't get anything for free in this world! It would be nice if you did, though. Wouldn't it? However, the reason why everyone is getting involved is that we are putting our panels on what we think are suitable roofs and in return, the homeowner gets to use as much free electricity from the panels as they like during daylight hours." The man listens to what it is I am saying but then tells me he needs to think about it. I do not argue. Instead, I say, "yes that's fair enough. A lot of people in the area also said that they want to think about it. The reason they told me they want to think about it was that they were not too sure on one or two things. What is it you are not sure about? Do you understand why the panels are free?" He replies: "I just want to think about it." I now think to myself that he is not interested but does not know how to say "no", or that he is unable to make a simple decision out of fear. I decide to fear of loss him to gauge his interest. I say, "ok that's fair enough. By all means, go away and think about it. However, we only come around every 18 months, and it may well be the last time we come around this area. I only have about a dozen slots left in the surveyor's diary, which won't take long to fill. It will be a shame if you miss out." I reconfirm that he is not committing himself to anything, but he still insists on thinking about it. I waste no more time. He is simply not interested, or he is just too afraid to make a decision of any kind.

I move on to the next door. I tell the man at the door that I am booking people in for surveys to see if their house qualifies for free solar panels. The prospect shouts, "solar panels are a rip off" and immediately shuts his door. Obviously, the word free has not registered!

I now go and speak to a middle - aged woman. I ask her how she is. She replies: "I am fine thanks, how are you?" I recognise this as a positive prospect. I explain what it is I am doing. She tells me a friend of hers just had solar panels installed, and she was thinking about it herself. This is an easy prospect, so I close her, and away I go.

The next house that I go to is the house that I knocked earlier in the day where the wife said her husband deals with everything. I speak to the woman again, and she tells me she asked her husband, and he is not interested. I ask her if he gave her a reason. She replies: "he is just not interested." I ask if it's possible to speak to him myself so that I can explain what it is we are doing. She says, "no" and again tells me that he is not interested. I know full well that she would not have explained it properly to her husband, but I have no option but to forget it and move on.

The next house that I knock, a woman answers the door. I explain what we are doing, and I hear a voice from inside the house saying, "we are not interested!" The wife explains that her husband is not interested. Again I forget it and move on.

The next door that I knock, a man answers but is not looking at ease, so I know that I need to relax the man fairly quickly if I have any hope of booking him for a survey. I explain that we missed him out, etc. He begins to relax as his curiosity takes over. "Missed me out for what?" He replies. I then tell him what we are doing. He looks interested and begins to lean on his door frame as I talk to him. This prospect could be a possible customer. He asks me what happens when you sell your house with the panels on the roof? I take this as a buying signal and answer his question. I now close the deal, but he tells me he needs to ask his partner. I ask if his partner is inside the house. He says, "yes," so I ask him if I can come in for a minute to explain it to his partner. I know he will be unlikely to explain it to her properly, which will inevitably lose the deal. He agrees. When I enter the house, I notice a picture on the wall, so I tell him it's a nice picture (relationship building). I then meet his partner and explain it to her. They both agree to go ahead, so I now have my third booking of the day.

It is now 18:30 and I only have a few more doors to knock. I pitch a woman on the door. She seems interested but says she will go and ask her husband. She walks away before I have a chance to ask her if I can speak to him. I hear her ask her husband: "are you interested in solar panels?" Surprise, surprise her husband says, "no." Shocked at what I have just heard; I tell the wife to at least say they are free. She replies: "I have asked him, and he is not interested, sorry." I have no option but to walk away.

The next door that I knock, a teenage boy answers. I ask him if his parents are there. He tells me that they are eating dinner. He asks me what it is about, so I explain that it's nothing serious, but that I think my colleague may have missed his parents out last week. I tell him that I will try and catch them another day. "What's the best time to catch them?" I ask. "Is Saturday a good day?" The boy tells me that both his parents will be home on Saturday, so I make a note and leave.

The next door that I knock, a woman answers the door. I can see her husband in the background, so I acknowledge him rather than ignore him. He now comes to listen to what I have to say. The wife tells me that she has heard that if you have a problem with your roof, then the company charges you to remove the system. She also asks me what happens if anything goes wrong with the system. I answer both questions and satisfy their concerns. I then close the deal and they both agree.

I knock a few more doors but all with no joy. They are just not interested, or they do not qualify. It is now 19:00, so I decide to go home. I have been knocking doors for four hours and have made £200 for the day. Bearing in mind that at the time of writing this book, the minimum wage is just under £7.00 per hour, meaning I would have had to work approximately 30 hours at the minimum wage to earn the equivalent amount of money that I have just earned. Sure, I've had to deal with some crap from people, but who cares? At the end of the day, I have hit my goal, and I have probably earned far more than anyone of the prospects who I have spoken to, and that's all because I have learnt to keep my attitude throughout the countless bullets of rejection.

CHAPTER 10
STORIES FROM THE FIELD

In this final chapter, I have decided to share some of my most memorable experiences from working in the field. Some are humorous, yet some just highlight the sheer stupidity of some people!

The Nutter Across the Road

I was working with someone who had been doing door to door sales for many years. We were out selling subscription television over in Birmingham and were speaking to a lady who had once been a previous customer when we noticed a middle - aged man come up the driveway. At first, we assumed that perhaps it was the lady's son. But before I knew it, the man immediately removed my badge from around my neck and told me he was going to ring the Police. Shocked at what he had just done, I followed him back down the drive to retrieve my badge, yet he just threw it in the middle of the road and then went into his house across the street. The lady who we were talking to looked equally shocked at what had just happened. Anyway, I grabbed my badge, and we then went to the next house. We then noticed that the man came out of his house again and began approaching us. He shouted at us to leave and then began to throw stones at us. By that time, we thought the man was just a complete nutter. He even squared up to the man I was with before the Police arrived. Once the Police had realised we were doing nothing wrong, they left us to it. No doubt they had stern words to say to the nutter who attacked us for no reason!

The Bully Policeman

I had not been in sales long when I had the unfortunate task of meeting this bully. I had knocked his door when selling phone and broadband, but before I could utter a word, he immediately and aggressively stepped towards me demanding I hand over my badge. He informed me that he was a police officer, and he could have me arrested if I didn't comply, so I handed over my badge. He then went back inside his house to confirm its identity. Once he had realised that it was genuine, he handed my badge back to me but with no apology. Obviously, he was under the impression that all door to door salespeople were crooks. Just as well I was not as ignorant and took the attitude that all coppers were bent!

The Loser with The Pretend Bad Leg

I was working on a council estate in Wolverhampton, West Midlands when I happened to walk by this scruffy looking man who was sitting on a wall with his girlfriend. He asked to use my phone so that he could ring home because he claimed that he had hurt his leg. I did not believe him for one minute and suspected he was trying to rob my phone. It was dark, and the area was deserted. I told him that I had left my phone in the car. He then asked to see what I had in the leather bag that I was carrying around my shoulder. I explained that it was just paperwork concerning my job. He demanded to have a look inside the bag, but when I refused, he became aggressive. He got off the wall and began to approach me demanding he takes a look in my bag. Again I refused. I then turned to walk away, but he started to get more aggressive, so I decided it was best if I just run away since I did not want to get into a fight on the field. He then ran after me down the road, at which point I turned around and said, "your leg doesn't look that bad now loser!"

The Angry Boyfriend

I knocked this door when a young lady answered. I explained that I was doing loft insulation for houses in the area. I told her I need to check her loft to see what current level of insulation she had. Once I had checked her loft, I could see that her current level of insulation was well below the recommended level, so I told her she would qualify to get insulated to the correct standards free of charge since she was claiming certain benefits. She agreed, so I began to fill out the paperwork. Just as I was finishing the paperwork, she received a phone call from her boyfriend, who she was supposed to pick up from the train station. She told her boyfriend that she was on her way and explained that she had someone at the house booking her in for free loft insulation. From the conversation, I could see that the boyfriend was not happy, so I asked to speak to him to explain. However, when I attempted to talk to him, he did not listen to a word I said but instead threatened me by telling me that he doesn't want loft insulation and that I better not be there when he gets back. The girlfriend was clearly embarrassed by her boyfriend's actions, but there was nothing she could do. The crazy thing is, is that I can guarantee he thought that it was going to cost him money. Just like a lot of people, he simply jumped to conclusions. In any case, I decided to cancel the order. After all, I would rather lose my commission than have a person like him benefiting from free loft insulation!

The Hyper Kids

I was working somewhere in the West Midlands area selling phone and broadband services. I knocked this door where a woman answered with two kids. I asked to go inside the house, which I later regretted! As I was trying to explain to the woman the benefits of my product, her two kids were running riot and jumping off the sofa and onto me. They were also swinging off my bag that I had on my shoulder. The mother obviously had no control over her kids. They were the most hyper kids I have ever come across, and I couldn't get out of the house fast enough! How anyone could cope with that is beyond me. The woman deserves a medal!

The Idiot with A Camera

I knocked this door when I was booking people in for surveys for the free solar panels. The man who answered immediately asked me what it was that I was selling. However, I made the mistake and said, "nothing," as technically I wasn't, but like most people he did not believe me. He then went on and shouted, "well I'll sue you if you are!" I replied: "Fine, now let me explain what it is I am doing!" As I began to explain what it was I was doing, I could see that he was clearly not listening to a word I was saying. He kept interrupting me, accusing me of being a liar! He kept repeating: "you liar, you liar!" He then, to my amazement, took his phone out of his pocket and started to film me as if he had caught out some crook. At that point, I just left. I had clearly made a mistake by spending any time with this individual since he was clearly not at all interested in listening and understanding what it was I was doing! He had simply jumped to conclusions and had made his mind up from the start that he was not going to listen to a word I said. If only he knew how foolish he was!

Foot Through the Ceiling

I was working in Coventry, West Midlands selling loft and cavity wall insulation. I knocked this door and got invited in to check the current level of insulation that was in the loft. While in the loft, I also checked the water tanks and took measurements so that I could work out the required amount of insulation. As I took the measurements, I shouted the measurements down to the prospect who was standing on his landing with a pen and paper. Then, just as I stepped from one wooden joist to the next, I accidentally missed the joist, and my entire leg went straight through the customer's ceiling! In shock at what had just happened, I attempted to regain my composure so that I could face the prospect who was now standing on his landing with my leg hanging from his ceiling. Fortunately, I was covered by insurance, and to my surprise, the prospect still decided to go ahead. In fact, he was more concerned about my leg than he was about his ceiling! From that day on, however, I never went into anyone's loft again. Instead, I just took the measurements from inside the house and only poked my head up through the loft hatch so that I could measure the depth of insulation.

The Prospect Who Thought Free Panels Were a Rip Off

I had the unfortunate task of dealing with this prospect. He immediately told me that he was not interested and began to shut his door. As always, I pretended to accept what he had said and went to walk away. As I walked away, I asked, "just out of curiosity, is there any particular reason as to why you are you not interested?" He replied: "you just cream off all the profits by selling the electricity back to the National Grid, and if there is anything left, I get it! It's a rip-off! I've already had 99 people come around about solar panels, and I am not interested!" To that, I couldn't help but laugh. I was not the least bit bothered if I booked him in or not because I already had a couple of sales under by belt and I really couldn't be bothered with this prospect. But since I had never actually heard anyone say this before, I asked him why he felt they were a rip off since they were not going to cost him anything! "It is free!" I said. He replied: "you don't get anything for free!" Still not the least bit bothered if I booked him in or not, I told him that he clearly did not properly understand how it worked, in which he shouted back: "I do!

Now go on, go on, stop wasting my time!" He then shut his door. You see this was a prospect who thought he knew it all, and because he was clearly a negative person, he thought negative about the product that I was representing. He was completely wrong in what he said, but he clearly thought he was so right and that I was a con man who was attempting to con him by selling solar panels, where he would receive very little benefit. The funny thing is, is that his very next door neighbour, along with a few others on the street, had our system installed. He obviously did not speak to any of those people, though. Now obviously the way I dealt with this prospect was the wrong way. By telling him that he clearly did not understand what I was doing - even though he clearly didn't, certainly did not help matters. What I needed to have done, was to have stroked his ego by telling him that he seemed well educated on that matter. That is if I could have said it with a straight face! Only then, when I had successfully calmed him down, could I have gently corrected him in what it was that I was doing! But then again, he was probably too far gone to deal with anyway!

The Moody Man in The Street

I was in the field when a speed walker, aged approximately in his 60's, was walking towards me. I decided to cross the road, but due to the traffic, I decided not to. However, as I turned back, I crossed the path of the speed walker, who at that time was about 3 metres away from me. As I did, he angrily shouted at me to "make my f**kin mind up." Shocked at what I had heard, I sarcastically said, "sorry." That, however, set him off with a whole load of verbal abuse. I did not bother to turn around, but I could hear him shouting at me as I was walking up the hill. It just goes to show how negative some people are and why you will always get some form of abuse when knocking people's doors on a daily basis. I can only be thankful that I never had to knock this man's door!

Prospect Who Just Couldn't Believe It Was Free

I spoke to this prospect who needed his loft insulated. He was claiming certain benefits, which meant he could get his loft insulated entirely free of charge. However, he refused to believe me that it was not going to cost him anything. I explained the reason as to why it was free was because the energy companies provided grants to meet emission targets set by the government. However, he was still very sceptical. I even wrote on the paperwork that the loft was to be insulated free of charge and under the column where it said: customer price, I wrote the amount of insulation required and filled in the price as £00:00. However, I could not phone the deal through to book it on because the office had just closed since it was Good Friday. Instead, I told him that I would come back the next day to ring it through. However, for some reason I was unable to return the next day, so I rang the prospect to cancel the appointment. When I rang the prospect, he still sounded very sceptical, and he told me that he rang up his energy provider asking about the grants for the insulation, but they told him that they knew nothing about it. Now obviously, he spoke to someone who knew nothing about it, but rather than waste any more time with this prospect, I told him that it's best if he doesn't get his loft insulated as he will only worry himself that there is a catch. Instead, I told him that he might as well just go and buy insulation from a DIY store since they quite often have good offers. He agreed, and that was that. I am afraid that some people are just too sceptical to deal with. In the end, it was simply not worth the time and effort on my part to carry on convincing him that it was free.

Prospect Who Thought That He Could Get Solar Panels Cheaper Than Free

I was working with someone up in the North West of England, when we knocked this door and a miserable looking woman answered. She immediately told us that she was not interested, even though she had no idea what it was she was not interested in. The husband then came to the door, so I explained to him that we were booking people in for surveys to see if they qualified to get free solar panels. However, he told me that he was not interested in solar panels and if he were, he would get them from the person living across the street who installs them. He told me they would be a lot cheaper than what we were doing them for. I asked him why he thought they would be cheaper. His reply was that if the company that we were representing had to pay us to come around, then ours are bound to be more expensive. At that point, I said, "well you are probably right" and just walked away. You see people will believe what they want to believe. There was absolutely no point in spending any more time with that individual since I could clearly see that he wasn't going to listen. Had he done so, then he may well have agreed to a free, no obligation survey to see if his house was suitable for completely free solar panels! It is so unfortunate that these type of people allow their ignorance to get in the way. By now he could have saved hundreds, if not thousands of pounds, on his electric bill, but he threw that all away all because he would simply not shut up and listen to the facts!

Prospect Who Said, "No" To Saving Over £700 A Year On His Telephone Bill

I was working in Castle Vale, Birmingham, where there are a large number of low-income households. I knocked this door and spoke to a woman who showed me her phone bill. It was

£80 per month due to a large number of international calls that she made to her son living in Australia. I explained that the phone company that I was representing could give her free international calls as well as free local and national calls 24/7, all for only £20 per month including line rental. She told me to come back later and speak to her husband. When I went back, to my amazement, her husband told me that he was not interested, and there was absolutely no way that he was going to change his mind. One would have thought that this would be a guaranteed sale. However, that was at the beginning of my days doing door to door, and I still had an awful lot to learn about people. What this taught me, was first, you can never come across as too eager because people become suspicious, and secondly, you can never rely on a call back, no matter how much of a dead - cert it may appear! I could knock another door where the saving may be minimal, but they could say, "yes." It's just the way it goes, I am afraid.

CONCLUSION

So there you have it! It is now down to you to put into practice what this book has taught you. Sure, it will still take time and persistence, but this book has given you all the secrets from years of experience knocking doors and has put you on the right track to earn a fantastic living as a canvasser. It has shown how complex people are, how ignorant people can be, but more importantly it has shown you how to overcome those challenges and successfully make a living as a canvasser. It will never be an easy profession - no matter what it is you are canvassing and regardless of whether the product is free or not. If only people could stop jumping to conclusions, stop believing in myths/negativity and instead make intelligent decisions based on facts, then not only would they benefit enormously from what you are offering, but dealing with people would be a pleasure. But then again if it weren't for people being people, then you would be unable to make the money that you can!

What's important is that you accept the field for what it is. Your goals need to be far greater than to allow yourself to get caught up with the day to day bull shit that you have to put up with. You will always win so long as you remain positive. Don't ever allow anyone or anything to take that away from you. If you can make up to £1000 in a week and as a result hit your goals, then who cares about all the people who were rude and ignorant? After all, it is them, and not you, that loses!

Good Luck & Happy Canvassing!

Made in United States
Troutdale, OR
03/25/2025